THE FIRST A[...]
ON LANCASHIRE

The Zeppelin Menace

Scott Carter-Clavell

AMBERLEY

To the memory of the those killed in the raid and to the bravery of previous generations, whichever side they were on.

We are not responsible for the past but are for the future.

What was it that we soldiers, stabbed each other, strangled each other, went for each other like mad dogs? What was it we, who had nothing against them personally, fought with them to the very end and death?
We were Civilised people after all. The Culture we boasted so much about is only a very thin Lacquer which chips off when we come into contact with cruel things like real war. To fire at each other from great distance, to drops bombs is something impersonal. But to each other's white in the eyes and to run with a bayonet against a man is against my conception and against my inner feeling.

Stefan Westmann

First published 2016

Amberley Publishing
The Hill, Stroud
Gloucestershire, GL5 4EP

www.amberley-books.com

British Library Cataloguing in Publication Data.
A catalogue record for this book is available from the British Library.

ISBN 978 1 4456 6342 5 (print)
ISBN 978 1 4456 6343 2 (ebook)

Origination by Amberley Publishing.
Printed in Great Britain.

CONTENTS

ACKNOWLEDGEMENTS

The author and publisher would like to thank the following people/organisations for permission to use copyrighted material in this book: Bolton Council, Bury Archives, Nordholz Aeronauticum, the Fleet Air Arm Museum and the Imperial War Museum for the use of photographs.

Every attempt has been made to seek permission for copyrighted material used in this book. However, if we have inadvertently used copyrighted material without permission/acknowledgement we apologise, and we will make the necessary correction at the first opportunity.

With grateful thanks to everyone who has helped with this book throughout its gradual creation and without whose input it would not exist: Jean Bell, Ann Bissett and Adam at Rawtenstall Library, Adam Carter, Birgitta Claus, Elizabeth Clavell (née Kenyon), Uncle Stan and Frances, Dr Anja Dorfer, Barbara Gilbert, Wendy Gradwell, Julie Lamara, John Leyland of Ramsbottom Heritage Society, Dennis Markuss, Cathy Moxon, Alan Murphy at Amberley Publishing, Alexander Peach, Andrea Percival, Brenda Richards of Ramsbottom Heritage Society, Julia Skinner at Francis Frith, Matthew Watson, the staff at Bolton Library, Museum and Archives, the staff at Bury Archives, the staff at Rawtenstall Library, the staff at Luftschiffe Aeronauticum Nordholz, the archive staff and volunteers at the Fleet Air Arm Archives, Ramsbottom Heritage Society, Professor David Wrench formerly of University of Bolton, Bury Collective, my parents and sister.

INTRODUCTION

I first found out about the Lancashire Zeppelin (LZ) air raid, many years ago, from my Great Grandma, who told me about it and of her father, who worked at Bessemer's Forge on Moor Lane in Bolton. Unfortunately, I don't remember too much of the story to relate. Through later research, this account was formed, and I hope that this will be of interest to those curious of this event of so long ago.

To solely focus on that night would not explain many unanswered questions as to the subject of Zeppelins and the so-called first blitz to younger generations for whom the war is but ancient almost disconnected history; therefore I include the first-hand experiences of the Germans and the British to try to give the Bolton raid a level of context in the depths of the First World War.

1916 advert for the Zepto Pencil.

CHAPTER 1

ZEPPELIN: MAN AND MACHINE

The Zeppelin was the invention of Count Ferdinand von Zeppelin, born on 8 July 1838. Interested in science and adventure, he flourished throughout a career in the army getting into many situations that earned him the nickname '*the crazy count*'. He retired in 1890, after declining the Kaiser's favourite regiment's victory in spring manoeuvres and threw himself into designing an airship. His interest in aeronautics had been steered towards balloons after a flight in a Union army balloon during the American Civil War.

The first Zeppelin was constructed in a floating hangar on Lake Constance. being revolutionary in design was named the LZ1. This was 420 feet long and 38 feet in diameter consisting of 24 aluminium girders making a rigid frame, the outer envelope covering the frame was woven from cotton. Sixteen rubberised cloth gas containers were suspended within the structure to hold 400,000 cubic feet of the lightest gas known, hydrogen.

LZ1's power source was two 8-horsepower motors driving two vertical and two horizontal propellers, controlled from a suspended gondola containing the engines, instruments and main crew. The primitive yet impressive LZ1's first flight was on 2 July 1900 and lasted just under 20 minutes. At 1,300 feet, the frame buckled leaving the craft drifting without steering. Even this primitive machine would dwarf modern jet airliners.

The shape of a Zeppelin was formed from the shape of its aluminium frame, braced with thousands of wires to hold the gas cells within the new aluminium alloy construction. Though at the time of LZ1's construction, there was only one company that produced aluminium in Germany. The lifting agent was hydrogen, the lightest yet most abundant element in the universe, making up about 90 per cent of the universe by weight, but is extremely flammable. This made airships extremely vulnerable, though igniting an airship proved to be more difficult than it sounds. So why not use helium? It is an inert gas – non-flammable while retaining the same lifting qualities of hydrogen. At this time in Germany, helium wasn't available, as it was tightly controlled in the US, which had a monopoly on its production from natural gas.

Yet hydrogen could be easily produced by industrial units, using the Messerschmitt method by passing steam over hot iron on site at Zeppelin bases and piped directly into the sheds. If contaminated by oxygen, this could be extremely dangerous, so very strict attention was paid to maintaining the purity of the hydrogen on bases.

To contain the gas was a difficult task, as early gas cells or ballonets could never hold enough hydrogen; the molecules could move through the weave of the cells. There then appeared to be a mixture of different types of gas cells being used until the outbreak of war, such as rubberised cloth, varnished fabric and Goldbeater's skin, the latter of which was found to be perfect.

Goldbeater's skin is the outside membrane of the large intestine of bovine species (cows, oxen). After slaughter, the membrane would be removed by hand and set to one side, it is a cylindrical bag of 0.5 m to 1 m long and about 0.1 m in diameter. It would require 15 of these skins to make one sq. m weighing about 130–150 g, 50,000 for one gas cell. The process of production was very simple, two pieces of the membrane, juxtaposed after treatment, overlapping by a few millimetres, would dry into a single layer. After it was complete, a second layer would be added creating a homogeneous double skin that was incredibly tight. It would take 250,000 membranes to make enough fabric for the gas cells in one wartime Zeppelin.

Due to the British blockade later on in the war, the Germans were forced to look for an alternative to Goldbeater's skins to make the gas cells within the Zeppelin. As there were not enough available, the intestine of cows were tested as well as pig's intestine. These different membranes were used in creating composite layers of the ballonet fabric.

Count Zeppelin was regarded as an eccentric by many in Germany, distrustful of his invention, over the next 14 years, during which the arms race between Britain and Germany reached full pitch. Donations from workers to Government officials went to the cause; a state lottery was created bringing in thousands of marks.

In 1905, LZ2 flew twice, though not for long thanks to a storm, and was quietly scrapped. This was followed by LZ3 in 1906, which managed a trip of 208 miles. This caused the Kaiser to overturn his previous discriminations against the count and awarded him the Order of the Black Eagle. The LZ3 satisfied the many witnesses and investors who watched the flights.

In 1907, the Reichstag passed a bill that provided subsidies for the construction of airships – amounting to 900,000 marks. The interest of the military quickly followed.

Ferdinand Zeppelin himself became a celebrity, and was invited to dinners and parties. Groups of admirers from all over visited him. He received an honorary degree from Tubingen University. On this occasion he made an aspirational speech.

If a man has this certainty and knows that he will reach his aim, it is not a virtue to find the way ... I am filled with hope and gratitude, for I am confident that the invention ... will become a blessing and asset for the German empire ... now,

Gentlemen do not smile, when I add that international laws will govern airship travel between all the peoples in the world.

The invention inspired many a commercial venture – Zeppelin-branded cigarettes were sold, medals were struck with the embossed face of the crazy count himself, coat manufacturers produced garments for flying, flowers were named in the inventor's honour and streets were renamed Zeppelin Strasse.

There was no equal in Britain that could counter this Germanic engineering as the propaganda machine was bolstered by the first commercial passenger airline DELAG (*Deutsche Luftschiffahrts-Aktien-Gesellschaft*). The Zeppelins built to carry passengers were named *Viktoria, Luise, Hanse, Sachsen, Deutschland* and *Schwaben,* were slow going at a majestic 45 mph but nonetheless airborne.

Pre-war Zeppelin postcard.

After a trip over Lake Constance in the LZ4 with the king and queen of Württemberg in July 1908, Count von Zeppelin was congratulated by the Kaiser on the initiation of a new national era – it was reported in the *New York Times* in an article entitled 'Zeppelin alarms Britain':

> The new era has had quite an effect in insular England, where the command of the air opens new and undesirable possibilities!
>
> That we may live to see the dirigible airship the accepted means of locomotion that the motor car is to-day, and then to all intents and purposes Britain will cease to be an Island.
>
> ... Germany's successes in aerial navigation have given the fatherland a tremendous advantage ... calls upon the German government to build a fleet of airships and aeroplanes at a cost of $1,000,000,000 and then transport an army of 350,000 men across the North Sea. England ... could be made to pay for her conquest by an indemnity of $5,000,000,000. ... programme such as this may seem to verge upon the realm of the fantastical ... as the feats accomplished by the Zeppelin airship point to ... upset for all existing plans for defending England from foreign invasion ... 'However reluctantly' says one newspaper 'England must contemplate the bridging of her moat by the opening of new roads through the air, and face the question of holding her own in that unsubstantial element.

German postcard making light of the enthusiasm for the Zeppelins.

These flew thousands of people all over Germany, whose enthusiasm for the Zeppelins was boundless regardless of accidents and mishaps. After the destruction of the LZ4 in 1910, contributions flooded in, following the accident. With the press coverage the fund swelled to 6,096,555 marks for a new airship to be built.

The DELAG Zeppelins gradually became famous and celebrated among the German public but the British were not so enthused. As tensions rose, it was believed that if a war were to occur, then the airships would be used against Britain. Articles in the British press did little to assuage any alarm, as reported in the *Daily Mail*.

> Out upon the glassy surface of Lake Constance the giant craft lies hidden in the floating corrugated-iron shed. Count Zeppelin's crews are at work inside, making various changes suggested by the successful trials. Count Zeppelin is confident he will be able to sail for an unbroken period of twenty-four hours. German military experts were exultant over the Count's recent achievements, and are bringing their utmost influence to bear to induce the government to purchase the ship without further experiments.

All over Britain, there were reported sightings of airships and Zeppelins over the country at various times, usually coinciding with reports in the press and bouts of imaginative interpretation of cloud formations and absolute conviction of a sighting, but in reality the airships were confined to the continent.

The true realities of the danger of this new technology were yet to be fully realised. It is an accepted risk of dealing with the new avant-garde that danger is an inherent part of the new machine. As at this time, flying either an airship or a more conventional aircraft was in its infancy, powered flight being less than a decade old.

Around the same time in Lancashire, it has been recorded that in Rossendale, the first recorded sighting of an aircraft was on 25 July 1911 when 'like the buzzing of a gigantic bluebottle' approaching from the direction of Accrington, the residents of Helmshore and Haslingden were transfixed by the sight of French Naval Lt Jean Louis Conneau, flying under the pseudonym Andre Beaumont in the *Daily Mail*'s Round Britain Air Race. His monoplane was described as looking like having the wings of an outstretched bird, in the local paper. Seventeen minutes later he landed in Manchester and the next day was the first competitor to reach Brooklands in Surrey to claim the £10,000 prize money.

H. G. Wells' novel *The War in the Air* appeared in 1908, imagining an attack on America by nearly a hundred Zeppelins that destroy New York as well as a battlecruiser fleet at sea. However fantastical it may seem, it illuminated the possibilities of these machines to the military minds on both sides of the English Channel.

As it would today, journalism easily contributed to the gradual inflation of the Zeppelins' reputation; although today it is hard not to view the fantasy with an element of humour, the seriousness of the latter sentiment could not be underestimated to the Edwardian Briton. The following year, the German military received its first Zeppelin.

In Britain's case, the article poses the critical question as to what advantage is it to command the sea if the enemy can fly over it? The empire covered a third of the globe, vulnerability of the home nation was concerning, as the arms race with Germany reached its peak.

In 1911, Germany was to openly claim that *Entente-Cordiale* had encircled them through the French treaty with Russia, justifying to themselves their own actions.

A year later, the DELAG Zeppelin crews had been made military reservists, the path to war for the Zeppelin was being laid out. Article 25 of the Hague Convention of 1899 stating, 'attack or bombardment by any means whatever of undefended towns or villages, dwellings or buildings is forbidden', which prohibited aircraft or balloons from dropping explosives in warfare was quietly forgotten.

The increase in size of the German Navy was a direct challenge to the Royal Navy, there was no other purpose for its creation. Between Britain and France, the Royal Navy patrolled the English Channel and the French Navy looked after the Mediterranean.

Due to the *Entente*'s arrangements in the German military mind, a total invasion of France would require the neutralisation of the Royal Navy in the Channel and North Sea. Information had seeped out regarding German intentions of 'the Schlieffen plan'. French Staff officers were in receipt of the plan to flank the French Army through Belgium, through their plan formulated in 1912 Number XVII.

In Britain in 1911, there was an investigation into the threat of the airships, resulting in the British constructing the R1 airship named *Mayfly* that had its back broken in a storm before ever taking off. The Royal Navy did eventually use Parseval airships – much smaller powered non-rigid balloon craft. In Germany, two types of airship were used during the war, Zeppelins by the Navy and Schutte-Lanz by the Army. It took six weeks to build one Zeppelin, as opposed to two years for a seagoing battleship.

The Schutte-Lanz was a wooden laminated plywood framed airship, whereas Zeppelins had a frame made from duralumin, an aluminium alloy.

Planning for a British air force began the same year primarily for reconnaissance, and by the end of 1912 the newly formed Royal Flying Corps (RFC) consisted of 12 balloons (from the Royal Engineers) and 36 aircraft, split into two sections between the navy and the army using the BE2 bi-plane. The embryonic force split in 1914, with the naval section forming the Royal Naval Air Service (RNAS) under the admiralty.

On the other side of the world, the *Argus* newspaper of Melbourne printed an announcement, in February 1914, that a joint German and English expedition by airship was going to take place to penetrate the Kaiser Wilhelm territory of German New Guinea, as yet uncharted territory. Stamps and postcards were produced in Germany to raise funds for the venture. Armed with six machine guns the trip was to be led by Lt Graetz, a seasoned flyer. Due to the outbreak of war, the expedition did not take place.

By the time of the outbreak of hostilities in August 1914, Britain had policed the seas for hundreds of year. The British Navy was a strong and two-power standard navy preserved at the standard equal to the next two largest navies in the world, together with the English Channel that had held potential invaders at bay. Now the means to bypass these defences had arrived which – this certainly hadn't gone unnoticed by either side. Despite fears, British Admiral Wilson predicted that the Zeppelins would not be able to navigate properly and find their way to the targets.

German propaganda of Zeppelins reaching London.

MEN OF LANCASHIRE.

(By Request.)

They have gone: all glad to go;
Men of Lancashire—Britons all.
They fear not to face the foe,
They have answered duty's call.
And yet daily others sally
From where the bonny hills sweep down,
Sweep down to Irwell's valley.

To France and to Belgium,
And e'en to Egypt some have gone.
Some have gone, and there are some
Who still long to follow on.
Brave men 'neath the flag do rally
From where the bonny hills sweep down,
Sweep down to Irwell's valley.

Living heroes—heroes dead—
Stern Lancashire may proudly boast.
Each of either, be it said,
Do yet count one of that great host
Which hath made a noble sally
From where the bonny hills sweep down,
Sweep down to Irwell's valley.

There's no need to tell the name
Of any one; no, nor the rank.
Each man's heart doth beat the same
Come he forth from mill or bank,
From wide street or narrow alley;
From where the bonny hills sweep down,
Sweep down to Irwell's valley.

Men from Burnley, Rossendale,
Ramsbottom, and men from Bury,
Men of Manchester more pale,
All unto our standard hurry;
Leaving Kitty, Nell, or Sally,
Just where the bonny hills sweep down,
Sweep down to Irwell's valley.

Kitty, she may be a wife:
Who has not heard of little Nell?
But Sally, oh! what a life
She used to lead her boy Cecil,
Before he made that sudden sally
From where the bonny hills sweep down,
Sweep down to Irwell's valley.

So may fortune favour all
The living brave now far away;
Some will stand, but some will fall
In the coming Spring-time fray;
Some there are who yet do dally
Where the bonny hills sweep down,
Sweep down to Irwell's valley.

R. PICKLES.

Edenfield.

'Men of Lancashire' poem.

CHAPTER 2

WAR

Within twenty-four hours of Archduke Franz Ferdinand's assassination, nine DELAG airships (eight Zeppelins and one Schutte-Lanz) were commandeered by the German Army and one Zeppelin taken by the Navy. In early August, military modification was put into full swing; wireless compartments, machine guns and bomb racks were fitted and markings painted on to the now lengthened airships.

At this point, all Zeppelins being laid down in the construction yards were for military use (primarily for the Navy) and existing peacetime craft were used by the Army.

The crews were also naval personnel, selected for their ability to work efficiently as a team, as well as their powers of endurance. After all, in what was to be a short European war, what better way than assert your authority over enemy countries with a long-range bombing machine that they could not equal or repel.

A completely new feature of warfare was about to begin.

On 6 August, Army Zeppelin Z6 bombed the Belgian city of Liege killing nine civilians. It dropped artillery shells rudimentarily adopted for aerial attack with streamer tails made of horse blanket to keep them straight in descent. Due to poor weather, Z6 was forced to fly low, flying near the Belgian fortress Lutetia. In the process, it was holed by rifle fire, and ultimately crash-landed in a forest near Bonn. On the continent, the use of the Zeppelins was initially confined to reconnaissance flights until there were enough to cover both recon and bombing missions.

By the time of the outbreak of hostilities, in 1914 Britain had a strong Navy, a small redoubtable Army and the RFC and RNAS of together less than 120 aircraft.

As became clear very quickly, civilians would not be exempted from the conflict with atrocity stories in the press and then from the thousands of Belgian refugees arriving in England. The British public were left in no doubt of barbarity in Belgium and France; the Kaiser's military would not let women and children stop the pursuit of their aims.

Airpower was now an undeniable part of warfare; Allied leaders and commanders were all too aware of this threat with the passing of the Defence of the Realm Act.

This was introduced to prevent the signalling or indication of landmarks to enemy aircraft. The first Zeppelin bombing mission with purpose-built bombs happened on the Eastern Front on 11 September on a railway yard at Viljka, near Vilna (now Vilnius).

On 5 August 1914, the First Lord of the Admiralty Winston Spencer Churchill deemed the RNAS responsible for taking on enemy air attackers on the mainland.

The culmination of a plan formulated by Churchill, anticipating the use of enemy airships towards the English mainland resulted in the RNAS unit at the front assisting the Royal Marines at Antwerp, being directed on 1 September to remain in France at Dunkirk to actively attack the airship bases with this order: deny the use of territory within a hundred miles of Dunkirk to German Zeppelins and to attack by aeroplanes all airships replenishing there.

As a result, on 22 September and 9 October 1914, attempts were made by the RNAS to bomb Zeppelin sheds at Cologne and Dusseldorf. The first attack bombed empty Zeppelin sheds, but the latter destroyed a brand new Zeppelin. Z9 along with its shed was destroyed in the first dive bombing attack in history by two Sopwith Tabloid aircraft piloted by Lt Marix and Cdr Grey. A German publicist, Rudolph Stratz, had been told early on in the war on how to be secretive about Zeppelin movements; however, after the war he wrote that he'd heard people on the high street in Cologne openly discussing Zeppelins based at the Dusseldorf base; therefore, he reasoned that this must have been overheard by enemy spies resulting in the raid on the town. It was also in September that restrictions on lighting were imposed in London, with street lamps painted over, shop signs and windows being dimmed, under threat of being fined.

On 21 November, four RNAS officers: Briggs, Babington, Sippe and Cannon prepared to attack the Fredrichshafen base using brand new AVRO 504s freshly arrived from the Manchester factory; three managed to take off without incident. The 250-mile trip was successful, the airship hangars were bombed and a Zeppelin damaged, though Briggs was shot down and taken prisoner. There were other raids on Cuxhaven as well.

These early attacks on the continent were the most effective form of defence in attempting to destroy the Zeppelins on the ground and in their sheds, albeit short lived. As the German Army airships suffered a large toll in the early months, it was the Navy that would operate from bases far beyond the reach of Allied airpower.

In the latter months of 1914, fears were realised, as it was reported that Zeppelins were flying over eastern England; Naval Zeppelin reconnaissance flights from Germany had spread out over the North Sea to examine the feasibility of extending offensive operations to the British mainland, German aerial power began to physically manifest itself in these trips over the east coast. In that now familiar tradition of UFO sightings, as they had before the conflict, many people believed they had seen a Zeppelin when they actually had seen a cloud formation and other atmospheric phenomena.

It was noted in the Periodical *Flight*, in September 1914, that on the continent, despite many German statements marking Zeppelin attacks over the Western Front, little had been seen or heard of Zeppelins during the first month and a half of the war, and that the RFC pilots operating daily reconnaissance flights have yet to spot one. The author of this article is very astute with his assessment of German intentions being only a matter of time.

> On the face of it, it seems curious that practically no use has been made of these huge craft of which the Germans, as we know, expected so much. It would … be foolish to assume that just because they have done nothing yet the Germans do not intend to make any use at all of them.
> When the time comes, to operate in conjunction with the German fleet. Alternatively, the Germans may possibly still consider that an aerial raid on the British coasts is feasible, and intend that it shall be carried out by the larger aircraft, while the smaller airships are attached to their armies … Germany has not built her Zeppelins for the mere purpose of allowing them to rot in their sheds. They will certainly attempt to use them, somewhere and somehow.

The British mainland did not escape for long, yet airships were not the first to attack the British mainland. In December 1914, a German naval squadron under Admiral Hipper bombarded Hartlepool, Whitby and Scarborough. The shelling killed 137 people without discrimination; wounding nearly 600. In Hartlepool, where the town was defended with naval guns and military, targets were hit and personnel killed. In Whitby and Scarborough where over 500 shells of various calibres were fired into the town, the 17 deaths, except one, were all civilians (ages 14 months to 65 years).

South Bay, Scarborough.

Scarborough was bombarded by German Navy.

Although apprehension and humour within the Allied populations towards these new machines was increasing, some elements within the German military had fairly low-held views (through a distrust of new technology) of the Zeppelin. Suggestions were even made that they should be simply used as scouts for the Uhlan cavalry during advances, which in reality is what they were used for in the initial months until a raid by Army Zeppelins on Verdun, Nancy and Dunkirk on Christmas day 1914. The Christmas truce of the regular armies in the trenches had not extended to the Army Airship Service.

Simultaneously, a German naval floatplane, a *Fredrichshafen* FF29 crossed the channel and flew up the Thames to the docks, a *Vickers Gunbus* FB4 pusher biplane appeared by chance and the visitor changed his mind swiftly retreating amid battery and machine gun fire. The two German occupants of the FF29 were awarded the Iron Cross the following day. On pusher aircraft, the engine was situated at the back facing rearwards, the pilot and observer would sit/stand facing forwards unhindered by the propeller in defensive fire.

With their Naval airship bases in northern Germany out of range of land-based Allied aircraft, there were few worries regarding vulnerability; though, being situated in this sanctuary gave rise to another problem in that they were ready and straining to take the war to England. The German Naval staff of the planning division's chief frustration was the Kaiser, who was afraid to directly assault the country with which he had so many ties. As a grandson of Queen Victoria, he was a regular visitor to Britain and his extended family in the preceding years. Incidentally, he had been bestowed the positions of honorary Field Marshal in the British Army, Colonel-in-Chief of the 1st Dragoon Guards and an Admiral in the Royal Navy; it was customary for other European royalty to hold positions in each other's services.

The Kaiser was ardently opposed to any attack upon Britain; Chancellor Bethmann-Hollwegg supported the Kaiser's stance clinging to the chance of a peace settlement with Britain.

Through the insistence of the Naval High Command and the chief of naval aviation *Kontoradmiral* Philipp on 7 January 1915, the Kaiser was impressed on by Admiral Hugo von Pohl to attack legitimate military targets in England while the weather would be favourable to long-range operations. The Kaiser reluctantly relented; eventual consent for air attacks on England was not given without condition: London was off limits, as it was a protected city under provisions of The Hague Convention, however it did contain military targets in addition to areas devoted to the output of war material.

The German High Command had a radically different view – a plan to burn London to the ground en masse using a fleet of Zeppelins, each armed with up to 300 incendiary devices, a strategic school of thought that evidently returned in 1940.

Gradually, areas of London were added to the target list; London docks on 12 February; east London on 5 May; followed by unrestricted bombing of London as of 20 July 1915.

Von Pohl added that Zeppelin commanders should take care not to damage private property or historical buildings if the attack was to take place.

In reality, when attacks were sanctioned the distinction between military and civilian targets was non-existent. Given the conduct of the Army towards civilians in Belgium, there were distinctions that ought to be respected rather than blurred at the discretion of individual commanders within the airship service; however, navigation and bomb aiming being so primitive, it would have been ridiculous to assume this was possible.

MAN'S DEVICES.

"He disappointeth the devices of the crafty, that their hands cannot perform their enterprise Job iv., 12.

In these dark days of sin and woes,
When nations are fighting against their foes,
When the cruel devices of sinful men,
Lay waste and destroy o'er field and glen;
Their devices are bringing cruel war,
Which this world ne'er knew before.

God shall disappoint their devices, whate'er the may be,
Whether devices to kill on land, or on sea;
Though hard they may fight, their hearts full of greed,
God, we know, is the stronger, and he will succeed;
Their lawless passions he shall destroy,
And reap on earth eternal joy.

When men just in the prime of life,
Should be shot down in terrible strife;
And the world in envious blood red rage,
Should in a terrible strife engage;
God grant that men possessed with ill,
Should cause no human blood to spill.

Restrain the craftiness of man,
If 'tis to do harm in our land;
To pillage, and murder, and put to flight,
Thy innocent children in pain and in plight;
Forbade, O God, again we plead,
That in man's heart should be such greed.

But the time shall come, as thou hast said,
And the tide of warfare that has spread;
O'er this, Thy land, with horror and with pain,
Shall be put down and peace restored again.
And the power of man to make warfare cease,
And the world be united with a lasting peace.

Bacup. GEORGE HARGREAVES.
November 2nd, 1916.

'Man's Devices' poem.

Rochdale camp soldiers.

CHAPTER 3

1915

This was the year it all changed. Far from the mobile conflict of 1914, unprecedented developments in technology and tactics set the benchmark for brutality and inventiveness.

On 10 January, the first raid plan was submitted to von Pohl by *Korvettenkapitän* Peter Strasser. It was an optimistic plan, not lacking in hubris, focused on military objectives on the Thames Estuary, Tynemouth, the Humber, Great Yarmouth, Lowestoft and Harwich. Three airships that would attack at dusk and return to base after nightfall.

Strasser was a strict officer convinced in the ability of the Zeppelin. He demanded his crew's devotion to their task; he himself was an example of having the blind confidence in technology, which through many an accident and storm had been proven to be deadly. Surmounting the North Sea barrier to England was without doubt worth risking those dangers.

The threat was certainly present but the fears and terror wrought on civilian populations compared to the amount of physical damage done were probably not justified after the initial attacks. The psychological effect of the Zeppelins evidently categorises them as an early 'Terror Weapon' of the air, an ancestor *in reputation* of the Junkers 87 *Stuka*, which screamed down onto Polish, French and British troops and civilians during the blitzkrieg, 25 years later. As in the perceptions of them, the vulnerabilities were also similar, being very vulnerable to fighter aircraft. Both machines lost the sinister reputation that had preceded them, as their weaknesses were exploited, rendering them almost useless due to superior tactics and technology.

Zeppelins were also a fair weather weapon. When the weather was calm it was described in Britain as a *Zepp* night, which made it sound all the more ominous. This meteorological injection of anxiety and fear into the civilian population by the threat was a useful side effect of the use of this new technology and was the aim of the German high command to elevate fears. It also benefited war profiteers, who started selling air raid insurance to businesses and property owners.

There was a lot of fear built up about these Zeppelins because of the publicity… the papers were supporting the idea that the Germans could demoralise us, the civilian population ... I can remember lying in bed frightened after hearing what might have been, only what might have been a Zeppelin overhead. Everyone exaggerated about them and that added to the fright, there wasn't one but a dozen overhead, so morally Jerry did have a very good weapon.

The publicity later on also had another effect: such was the presence of the Zeppelins through the newspaper that advertisers used it to their full advantage, selling products to those seeking protection, shelter or entertainment while an air raid was in progress. Insurance for air raids, blackout curtains, Zeppelin-shaped pencils, ointments and cures; if a product could be portrayed as a counter to the threat of airships then it would be.

The first Zeppelin attack on Britain occurred on the night of 19 January by Zeppelins L3 and L4 (early types with open gondolas). On Great Yarmouth and Kings Lynn, 25 bombs were dropped, killing Samuel Smith and Martha Taylor first, as well as 2 others, with 13 injured; £8,000 of damage was inflicted. No military targets were hit.

As trench warfare settled into a savage slogging match, other aspects of this unprecedented war appeared.

In March, the unrestricted sea blockade of Germany began as a result of the U-boat attacks on shipping: a declaration that they would sink every ship presumed to be British. Airships were the perfect tool to skip over the world's largest navy attempting to cease the flow of food and raw material into German ports. The British, therefore, began to impact upon the German population without flying over it, but by patrolling at sea, stopping the badly needed goods. In 1914, the German government was confident that the country could produce 90 per cent of its own food; although, this was aided by millions of tons of imported corn, barley, oats and fertilisers. Not long after the war started, problems began to appear that led to the unrelenting shortages for German civilians by 1918. This, throughout the war, certainly had more impact on the German civilians than the Zeppelins had on the British people.

On the 22 April, the Germans used poison gas for the first time on the Western Front against the French 45th Algerian Division and 78th Division troops near Ypres. The wind blew the poison gas drifted into the trenches, dug-outs and funk-holes of the unsuspecting troops. A 4-mile section of organised regiments disintegrated within the greenish-yellow cloud between the British and Belgian armies, as hundreds of French and colonial troops died in horrifying circumstances or managed to flee. The advancing Germans found no resistance and dug in; it took weary Canadian battalions to push them back, being attacked with the new gas in the process and suffering 6,000 causalities by the end of the week. This weapon would be a regular feature of warfare. On the Western Front, there was a continuous development of the gas on both sides, and both desperately needed masks.

That same month, Zeppelin L9 under the command of Heinrich Mathy bombed countryside in the north-east at Wansbeck in Northumbria. He had selected Tynemouth docks as a target after a fruitless ship-hunting mission over the North

Sea. He had missed the docks by miles but reported that he had inflicted great damage to them.

Raids were becoming frequent and it was noted by the meteorologically minded that, certainly in the regularly visited areas, raids were occurring when the barometer was registering high pressure.

On 7 May at 2.10 p.m., U-boat U20 torpedoed the large unarmed Cunard liner *Luistania* sailing from New York along the south coast of Ireland. A total of 1,119 civilians died including men, women, children and babies from neutral countries; a total of 764 survived. The absolute horror of this act spread around the world, with rioting in many cities internationally targeting German-owned business and those with foreign-sounding names.

However, the German attitude to the sinking was that the ship had been carrying illegal munitions for the British government; therefore, anyone travelling on it did so risking their lives, and to this end adverts had been placed in New York newspapers days before the *Lusitania* sailed from New York on 1 May, warning passengers not to travel due to the unrestricted submarine attacks on any vessel flying the Union Jack.

Then on 31 May 1915, Zeppelin LZ38 flew high in cloud over London and commenced a bombardment, the airship remained unseen throughout causing 8 deaths, wounding 35, and much destruction. One of its first victims was three-year-old Elsie Leggatt in Cowper Road, Stoke Newington, who burned to death in her bedroom after her family had evacuated the stricken house, believing in the confusion that a neighbour had taken Elsie outside. Her 11-year-old sister Elizabeth died of her burns a few days later. The horror continued with explosives and incendiaries being dropped.

A married couple Henry and Caroline Good were trapped by fire from an incendiary in their bedroom and their bodies were found kneeling together by the bed as though in prayer with Henry's arm around his wife's shoulder with Henrys arm around his wife's shoulders.

Sylvia Pankhurst witnessed the explosions:

Huge reports smote the ear, shattering deafening, and the roar of falling masonry... The thought of the bombs crashing down crashing down on the densely populated city was appalling.

Count Zeppelin however stated in an interview to the well-travelled Berlin Correspondent of United Press, American Karl Henry von Wiegand after raids had started on England...

No one regrets more than I do that non-combatants have been killed, but not have non-combatants been killed by other weapons of war as well ... Why is England pouring forth this cry of outrage just now? Actually, England is feeling so outraged because she is afraid that the Zeppelins might destroy her 'splendid isolation.' The English are outraged furthermore, that they have not succeeded in constructing anything like the Zeppelin.

Zepp nights became a regular event for those in the south and east of England. The British public's curiosity was raised. When raids occurred, crowds would gather to watch the spectacle of the raider passing over, if the bombs weren't dropping too near. As innocent casualties mounted, the public began to see and feel the very nature of industrialised modern warfare as houses were destroyed; the horrifying deaths of people of all ages and walks of life in their own homes, on the streets, in school and at work by shrapnel, shock, concussion, burns, evisceration, decapitation and lacerations. It appears the spirit of the British people was strengthened with the resolve to carry on as the war had already made huge changes to life, the raids were another part of that and something that had to be endured.

For blackouts in London, there was a plan to notify the population by means of centrally turning off the electricity supply when a raid started. The more ominous way of notifying the people was adjusting the domestic gas pressure. As the majority of homes had gas lighting, the pressure would rise and fall twice, signifying that blackout restrictions were to be observed. Although it was not a standardised practice, air-raid drills varied from town to town. However, as we shall see, some areas as yet not molested by the airborne menace had yet to adopt air-raid warning measures.

Hopes flourished on 7 June, when Sub Lt Warneford flying a Moraine-Saunler monoplane attacked an Army Zeppelin LZ37 over Belgium, initially with machine gun fire to no effect. Then he dropped a bomb on top of the airship, which exploded, ignited the hydrogen and sent it down burning. The blast knocked out Warneford's engine for a short time, and landing behind enemy lines he managed

A raiding Zeppelin caught in a searchlight as shells burst nearby.

to restart it and return home unscathed to be awarded the VC. Unfortunately, he was killed along with an American journalist in a flying accident 10 days later.

In July, the first flamethrower attack was made against British troops in a nightmare assault at Hooge.

Two days after English nurse Edith Cavell was executed at the *Tir Nationale* by the German Army in Brussels on 14 October, London was struck again. The outrage was reaching fever pitch. L15 and other Zeppelins dropped bombs at random. An omnibus was hit killing the driver and passengers at Aldwych. In one theatre, the Gaiety, explosions outside led many of the performers and audience alike to seek safety. As the crashes outside went on, a Mr Leslie Henson, one of the night's acts, struck up the Orchestra into a tune and led a lively dance with the girls in their flimsy costumes until events calmed down. Yet, outside the entrance, a 15-year-old pageboy had been blown to pieces next to the front door while sharing a cigarette with his friend who, in the strange way of explosions, survived. In total, 17 people were killed and 21 injured.

Heinrich Mathy to Karl von Weigand after a raid on London:

> Now, for the first time, my instructions were to attack certain points in the downtown City of London, such as railway stations, bridges, industrial establishments. Strict orders to do everything possible to avoid hitting St. Paul's and other churches, museums, Palace, Westminster Abbey, Parliament, and, of course, residential districts.
>
> I want to say there's not an officer or man in the aerial fleet who doesn't feel it as deeply when he learns that women and children and other non-combatants are killed, as does a gunner or commander of big guns when he hears his shell didn't strike exactly where he wanted it to, and resulted in the death and injury of non-combatants. In fact, I would much rather stand on the bridge of a torpedo-boat, fighting ship against ship, than attack a city from the air, although not because the danger to me is much greater in the latter.

The branding of German *Kultur* (culture) became an insult as a culture with primary instinct for wanton violence and acts of cruelty. For the Zeppelin's raids, the public, all too aware of the threat, would soon turn to anger that would force the government to retain war material otherwise headed abroad: such as guns, aircraft and personnel. Not all of his countrymen privately shared the same view of bombing, Admiral Von Tirpitz wrote to his wife:

> I contend for the standpoint of an eye for an eye, but I am not in favour of the evil policy which is lately gaining vogue, I mean the policy of 'frightfulness'. The indiscriminate dropping of bombs is wrong; they are repulsive when they kill and maim children and old women, and one can too soon grow callous to such wanton cruelty. We should not be so opportunistic as to stoop to our basic instincts

Then fear became reality, the first war in Europe since the defeat of Napoleon had become stuck when each side tried to knock the other out in the bloodiest examples of strategic trial-and-error ever committed.

Rochdale Territorials at Edgworth Camp near Bolton, 1914–42.

CHAPTER 4

HOME DEFENCE

The unabating air raids fuelled fearful angry reactions of British populations and was not exactly an advantage for the Germans. There were incidents where RFC personnel and property were damaged in return for what was seen as paltry efforts of defence from the raiders. This forced the government to act, although at this point there simply were no methods of detecting, tracking and scrambling aircraft towards the intruders.

In one area, an RFC aerodrome was seen to send aircraft up in daylight and not at night. In reality, it was a training centre for new pilots but to the public, it was another sign of inaction, a failure to defend them. This fervour pressured the government to redirect resources to bombed areas for reassurance, which in an embryonic way started the build-up of the home defence system.

The German population had reacted with fascination and excitement, but for the majority of the British population a few years previously the sight even of an aeroplane would be a memorable occasion; a decade previously it would have been the motorcar. A craft the size larger than an ocean liner passing high overhead certainly would have fuelled fears, speculation and undoubtedly fanciful exaggerations. With the Zeppelins, many people appear to have been more awe struck than really frightened, perhaps hoping that this unwelcome event would soon be over. As one eyewitness put it, after all, some people were still talking about the Boer War.

It did certainly capture the imaginations of children, inevitably becoming part of games, as in one instance, which was widely reported in the national press. It was humorously dubbed *Zeppelinitus*, as some children had taken a game to another level, when at Wycombe, in December 1916, two boys had been caught standing on a railway bridge, playing at being Zeppelins, dropping bombs (stones) onto the trains hurtling past underneath.

The viability of it being the harbinger of impending death on a large scale was just too present as a possibility to be trivialised. They appeared as the 'unseen monsters of the dark' who could strike anywhere at women and children; unlike the U-boat menace that was confined to the sea, the word '*Zepp*' became a slang for the sinister threat, and, after a few raids, the words grew into more hateful forms such as 'the baby killers'. As the casualties mounted, the name was not inaccurate. Their strange, almost surreal appearance lent credence to a horrific reputation in the great Edwardian imagination.

The renowned Zeppelin Cdr Heinrich Mathy was interviewed by Karl von Weigand. The article, from the *New York World*, was republished in the *Flight* magazine in England in October 1915. There is a disclaimer fronting the article stating that many of the described facts in it are ludicrous stemming from a man whose 'recent visit to London scattered Promiscuous murder around Women, Children and non-combatants'.

> KvW: What could a fleet of twenty-five or more Zeppelins do in an attack on London? ...
>
> HM: If you mean an attack without consideration for anything or anyone, that would be terrible, awful ... when we have to pick out certain points. Such a fleet could probably cause more than a thousand fires, and would mean the destruction of the greater part of London; but I don't think there is any danger of that. We have no wish to destroy indiscriminately or to injure and kill women, children and other non-combatants.

Fuhrer de Luftschiffe Peter Strasser in a letter to his mother describes his clearly ardent feelings on being labelled a 'baby killer' and clearly justifies to her his actions and that of his men.

> We are enjoying pleasant weather here, and we are marching against England ... We who strike at the enemy where his heart beats have been slandered as 'baby killers' and murderers of women. Such name calling is to be expected from enemy quarters. It is maddening to learn, however, that even in Germany there are simple fools and deluded altruists who condemn us ... What we do is very necessary. Nowadays there is no such animal as a non-combatant; modern warfare is total warfare ... You and I mother, have discussed this subject, and I know you understand what I say. My men are brave, their cause holy, so how can they sin while doing their duty?

Strasser's conviction was absolute, his devotion to his duty, airships and men unflinching. Nothing would hinder them, even civilians, as had been the case in Belgium – it is as much as a confession that certainly at officer level it wasn't a necessity to adhere to the Kaiser's will, absolving his crews of any accusation of wilful murder of children. He was not necessarily alone in that view; the King of Wurttemberg gave a dinner speech in September 1916:

> It is against England that our principal efforts must be directed. Every Zeppelin that drops destruction on London is an instrument of righteousness. England must be attacked more and more from the air, since our glorious armies which annihilate all other enemies cannot reach the shores of our most dangerous foe.

British troops at the front heard about the raids through newspapers and letters. Here a Pte G. Bell of the 9th Bn, Army Cyclist Corps recounted an encounter with a captured German pilot in a POW camp in France:

> The first thing you did if you got hold of a Jerry was to see what you could get of him – if he'd a watch or anything like that ... None of the scruffy ones that came into our camp had anything that was worth having ... There was a lot of talk of Zeppelin raids and the Jerries' bombing London and killing a lot of civilians and, just at that time we had a Jerry airman who'd been brought down. He was handed over to us and one of my mates interrogated him. He tried to find out whether he'd been over, dropping bombs. He said, 'If he's been over *there,* I'll shoot him! He'll never get away!' He would have done too! Life meant nothing to you. Life was in jeopardy ... it brutalises you, war does ... All you're doing is looking after your own skin all the time. Head down.

Early in 1915, the RNAS had more aircraft than the RFC, mainly concentrated at small fledgling aerodromes in the Home Counties and East Anglia. For the British pilots, it was found to be a great difficulty locating the intruders once they were airborne. It depended on visual contact at night in varying cloud conditions, and this resulted in many defensive sorties never locating the raiders. It had been proposed in June of that year by the director of home defence Gen. Launcelot Kiggell that the RNAS was to deal with raiders off the coast and the RFC deal with the raiders inland. This was eventually formally agreed on 22 February by the governments war committee.

On 31 January 1916, 436 bombs were dropped by 16 Zeppelins, including 60 bombs on London; 4 people were killed and 12 injured, experience was increasing for the Zeppelin crews, civilians and home defences.

British soldiers.

The newspaper *Leipzig Neueste Nachricten* trumpeted about the London air raids with raving fervour, leaving readers in no doubt as to their feelings of air raids!

London, the heart which pumps lifeblood into the arteries of the degenerate nation, has been mauled and mutilated with bombs by brave German fighting men in German airships ... the long yearned-for punishment has befallen England, this people of liars, cynics and hypocrites, a punishment for the countless sins of ages past. It is neither blind hatred or raging anger that inspires our airship heroes, but a religious humility at being chosen the instrument of God's wrath ... When they saw London being consumed in smoke and flame, just as Sodom was burned by fire from heaven to requite the wickedness of its people.

Under the assaults, London received the bulk of the available defences, the north was drip-fed material; though, it was not until a raid on Hull, in March 1916, that efforts were stepped up and the northern home defence gradually evolved slowly, as even by mid-1916 there were roughly 200 guns and an equivalent number of searchlights available for the country, though double had been planned for.

It is clear that more civilian areas suffered than industry or military targets from Zeppelin raids, and there was only one attack that caused the largest number of military deaths in an air raid. At Cleethorpes in the early hours of 1 April 1916, Zeppelin L22 bombed a Baptist Chapel occupied by 70 members of E company, 3rd Bn Manchester Regt. Bombs hit the roof, which caused its collapse and that of a wall onto neighbouring shops in which A company were quartered. A total of 31 deaths occurred, with 50 people being injured, much assistance was given by the VAD ladies in extremely difficult blackout conditions, with the Town hall being used as a casualty station.

L15 was the first naval Zeppelin to be brought down over England; anti-aircraft guns fired shrapnel shells that shredded the gas cells, coming down due to loss of hydrogen when it splashed into the Thames Estuary.

Though under fire, navigation and perceptions of distance became even more disjointed, as described by Lt Kuhne, who as officer of the watch accompanied *Kapitanleutnant* Breithaupt on L15's last mission over London in April 1916:

It is a clear night. London lies wrapped in the blackest darkness. We can see nothing at all; suddenly, we come under heavy fire … it made feel devilishly queer when those pale fingers of light refused to let go of us. We knew they were working out our height and speed … we were about 2,500 m up … not the slightest wisp of cloud … I am lying in the catwalk close to the entrance of the bow car with my eyes fixed to the telescope. Those damned searchlights down below … we get a salvo. Shrapnel's; they hit us amidships, I am tossed up off the floor by the shock … certainly we have done our job … it is up to us to get the ship home … What Port … Where is East Frisia? Where indeed … we continue to drop … The signalling petty officer reports 'height 400 metres'. 'Albrecht, how far are we off home?'… '250 Kno—' He cannot finish the word; an ominous crack resounds through the whole ship. We are in pitch darkness … I cannot even feel whether we are still falling.

After L15 hits the water, it starts to settle. The crew climb out of the gondolas and climb onto the wreck.

Where are we? A general shrugging of shoulders answers the questioner. Who knows? If we're lucky we may be somewhere near our picket boats … Shadows of Trawlers loom out of the night. Dutchmen? We slit the few gas bags that still contain gas, the L15 must sink. The Dutchmen are no Dutchmen. They are Englishmen.

Unbeknown to them they had gone into the Thames Estuary.

A major factor in the coordination (or lack of) in Zeppelin attacks was navigation being under-developed by modern standards – though it is important to view them in the context of the time. Certain methods were employed, some of which were to be developed over time and some that died with the Zeppelin. Dead reckoning was tried and trusted by aircraft crews at this time.

With the advent of Britain's Department of Regulatory Agencies (DORA) regulations as of 8 August 1914, no lighting was allowed on the ground so as to hinder enemy airships; crews used whatever was visible to find a target. Occasionally, when a Zeppelin was reported in an area, people tried to extinguish the gas lamps that lit the streets. It has also been recorded that, when it was over Lincolnshire in mid-1916, a Zeppelin followed a bus's headlight to a village and when the bus stopped, the Zeppelin started to bomb the area.

In the generally calm and clear conditions of a '*Zepp*' night, it seemingly wasn't initially understood that the landscape below in the light of the moon would be very visible – the nocturnal trains, beacons with glowing cabs chuffing out long clouds of grey–white smoke would simply be a convenient guide to lead raiders to towns and cities.

Flying at height at night obviously had its perils, one for crews operating over England was that the maps they were issued for the trip contained black crosses on towns that were not to be attacked.

Trying to avoid these towns would be more luck than anything else; in ideal daylight conditions, it still would contain a degree of uncertainty. The only real certain target was London, as it was so large, and coastal ports and estuaries that were at prominent points; otherwise, many large anonymous industrial towns, small villages and large areas of unlit countryside were without many distinguishing landmarks.

The slightly more accurate yet hazardous alternative to spotting from the Zeppelins gondolas itself was to lower the 'Cloud/Observation Car' or *spahkorb* by hand winch.

This was a 14-foot-long covered-in device that had been through various stages of designs since March 1915. The later versions such as the Mark Six had a window, constructed of celluloid, in the nose; an electric reading light; a wicker chair plus map board; telephone; and compass. This was attached to the Zeppelin by 750–1,000 m of cable – some of which was hollow, for running the telephone and electricity cables.

There are various accounts that differ over the popularity of this station – it was the only place where crew could smoke a cigarette. Although, I would imagine on manoeuvring the airship, any sort of swing or pendulum effect must have been sickening and terrifying for the man in it. The observers were to indicate targets to the captain as well as picking out landmarks. In two instances, cloud cars were found on the ground with yards of cable attached, one with a dead observer inside. It would have been a situation to be inside if the Zeppelin needed to ascend rapidly, there was a distinct possibility that the cloud car would be cut free if it was really urgent; this would give the Zeppelin extra lift.

On board a Zeppelin, the wireless operator would have had to wind out the aerial and transmit messages by using a Morse key. A regular job he had to do was to decipher the meteorological messages with a weather-key and note them for the Officer of the watch to enter onto the weather chart. These messages were sent along with orders and reports by standard wireless stations. The special stations that dealt solely in navigation transmissions sent bearings out to raiders over England or the North Sea; they were emitted from three stations at bases in Germany at Nordholz, List and Tondern, and one in Bruges. They all took down wavelength notes sent by the airship then transmitted the cross-bearings back to the airship. These would be drawn onto a chart, where lines intersected would be the airship's position. This system was highly susceptible to weather and atmospheric disturbances creating noise in the operator's headset.

Not only did this crude system have a margin of error of many miles, but it also assisted the British in tracking the Zeppelins with surprising accuracy, by listening in and disrupting its frequencies. It was also a slow process, if there were many requests from different Zeppelins, then they would be added to a list, which would be worked through gradually despite the pleas from wireless operators for a position.

After the war, Baron von Buttlar Brandenfels recounted his experiences of commanding Zeppelins, including an example of the lack of accurate navigation over England.

We had been to England in the L30, but on the homeward trip we went wrong in our navigation. We dropped bombs on some English batteries but we had not the slightest notion of their position. On the following afternoon I wrote out my report, but omitted the name of the town where we had attacked the batteries. A painful inevitable necessity... In a Hamburg bar we wracked our brains to find out where we had wandered to in England ... we heard them calling out a special edition of the paper ... and we read there in black and white that only the previous night L30 had carried out a most successful attack on Maldon ... the paper apparently knew more than we did ... I instructed my clerk to put Maldon in the space on the report ... and four weeks later I received official recognition for 'accurate navigation.

Former Zeppelin crewmember, Kurt Dehn, later acknowledged, 'So called targets were no targets. They thought they were over the estuary of the Thames, and in reality they were near Portsmouth'. Bombing was almost random, 'it is rubbish to say that this was the so-and-so building and we dropped our bombs over that building. You were happy enough if you found London, and even happier if you could drop your bombs and go home as soon as possible'.

Working in a Zeppelin was extremely arduous for the crew, who were naval volunteers (all were officers or NCOs); these had to prove their camaraderie, responsibility and initiative in addition to their resistance to the intense cold and wet conditions they were to have to endure; with at times, having to cope with air depravation. They all had passed tests to ensure their steadfastness, good eyesight together with good nerves, heart and general health.

I was the elevator man on the L.13, Lieutenant Heinrich Mathy was our captain ... The captain ordered we increase our altitude to 2,500 metres, so I spun the elevator wheel bringing the nose to a slight upwards angle and carried on. It was cold. It was so cold that our sandwiches had frozen in our pockets and our eyebrows had turned white with the frost. We'd all got fur-lined suits but they didn't keep out the cold at that height and we were all shivering but Mathy didn't seem to notice.

The Commander would be based in the gondola at the front, as well as the radioman who would be working in his soundproof room, shielded from the noise of the engine powering the propeller at the rear of the gondola.

There would be elevator and rudder men at the helm positions near the front, side machine gunners and an executive officer, who would have to operate the bombsight and transfer orders around the airship. Any man leaving the gondola would have to climb out a hatch on in the roof and carefully climb up an exposed ladder before entering the hull of the airship and the relative stability of the internal gangway roughly 170 m (550 feet) long.

The outer cover of the hull was a light cotton that had been painted with clear dope to taut and waterproof the fabric. Inside, amid the thousands of bracing wires and aluminium girders, a gangway ran the length of the bottom of the ship to allow access for the crew to every position including to the ladders that would lead to the machine gun pits built on the front top and rear hull.

The front gun-pit ladder was just forward of the control gondola going vertically upwards – for nearly 19 m or 62 feet until reaching the gunners' position. In the darkness, amid gas cells and anti-aircraft (AA) fire, this would have been an arduous climb.

Inside the hull next to the gangway, there were bombs on racks over hatches that would be electrically released from a panel at the front of the control gondola. Immediately forward of the 'after' gondola, there would be the cloud car station, with the cable-winding mechanism as well as small fuel and oil tanks positioned at intervals along the gangway, with many small pipes running up down and along inside.

Within the rear 'after' gondola was the warmest place for the crew, as this is where three engines were. This was very noisy, with stench of fuel and oil. Some mechanics fitted hot plates to the engines exhaust manifolds to thaw their rations before eating them. On early trips over France, it had been found that oil had frozen in the tanks causing huge difficulties, as the pipes and tanks were not protected from the cold.

Johann Brama, a former helmsman aboard *M.IV*, wrote a memoir about hunting a submarine in the Baltic Sea in 1915. *M.IV* was an army ship utilised for naval use:

> Before dropping our bombs, we had to rise at least another 200 metres to avoid the powerful effects of the air-pressure. 'Full throttle ahead, and helm hard a-starboard!' was the order ... we needed several minutes to complete our loop. Would the Submarine dive down during that time? ... Our loop was at least 1,000 metres long, and the wind was drifting us away from our objective ... At last we were over the submarine again.

Calm weather for Zeppelin operations did not mean amenable conditions for the crew. Once they were aloft, the temperature would plummet. On most trips, any man touching metal with his bare hands would find them almost burned by the cold or stuck to metal fittings or the structure. The later airships flying above 10,000 feet required bottled oxygen for crews, so rudimentary mouthpieces and tanks were fitted.

On missions, the crew would forego the strict uniform procedures of ground duty and wear many layers, thick coats, gloves, scarves, felt boots and goggles.

Crew numbers varied according to the size of the Zeppelin. L21 had 17; each man had his own assigned duties: in addition to the navigator; two petty officers – to handle the elevator controls; two petty officers – to control rudder operation; two wireless operators; one petty officer as sail-maker in charge of the gas cells and outer cover; two machinist's mates for each engine.

On operational missions some members might be left behind to lighten the load. When off duty, the respective crewmembers would alternate on watch at various points and machine gun positions.

> We didn't have anything to fear from the British planes. Their pilots weren't experienced night fighters and we had little to fear from the guns. They weren't likely to hit us at that height and if they did they wouldn't have done much damage other than make a hole in the envelope or puncture the ballonet and we had a sail-maker who could repair this while were flying. I wouldn't have wanted his job; having to scramble through the rigging and work at that height and in those conditions and he could only use one hand to support himself because he had to carry all the tools of his trade in the other, the rope with which to mend the tears, the needles and material.

In terms of bombs carried, the airships would carry a real mixture of sizes of explosives (Carbonit) and incendiary (Brandebombe). The early incendiaries were conical in shape but these were developed into a tall straight canister design – both using the technology of Hans Goldschmidt, the inventor of the thermite welding process.

Early Conical Type

Ready to Drop

Part Burned

Burned to Core

The Goldschmidt incendiary had a metal cylindrical core of thermite with a percussion cap fuse at the base, surrounding this core was another compartment of thin metal containing benzol, a solidified oil. Covering this section was a tarred rope; at the top there was a hook for stowage on-board. Once dropped, theoretically, the fuse would ignite the thermite, burning at 2,500 degrees in an exothermic reaction, in turn igniting the benzol, in turn igniting the tarred rope, which would keep burning for a while longer. If not checked, it would in a very short space of time become a conflagration. The reliability certainly was haphazard for this type of bomb and many did not burn or ignite properly, but many did.

Cylindrical Type

The Carbonite explosive bomb, named after AG Carbonit the manufacturer, came in different sizes, but generally were of the same design, until 1916, when large torpedo shaped PuW aerial bombs began to be adopted for use with fixed-wing aircraft and army Zeppelins, as Carbonit bombs were deemed obsolete. However, the Carbonit bombs were the first to be equipped with tail fuses that armed through a propeller wind milling on the rear, after being released over a target.

Aiming the bombs was the responsibility of the executive officer, and he operated the bombsight made by Carl Zeiss, which was supposedly a quite accurate device. Settings would be made with the altitude and by measuring the speed of the airship, although if altitudes and courses were changed and bombs dropped, accuracy would suffer, but it would very much depend on the skill and experience of the officer looking at the target and operating the bomb release switches.

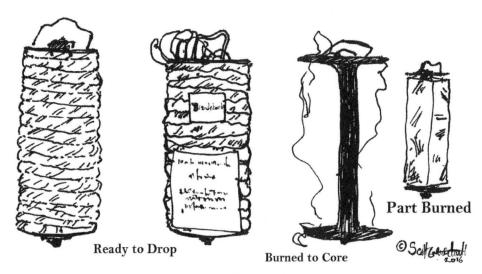

Ready to Drop   **Part Burned**

Burned to Core

𝕭𝖗𝖆𝖓𝖉𝖊𝖇𝖔𝖒𝖇𝖊

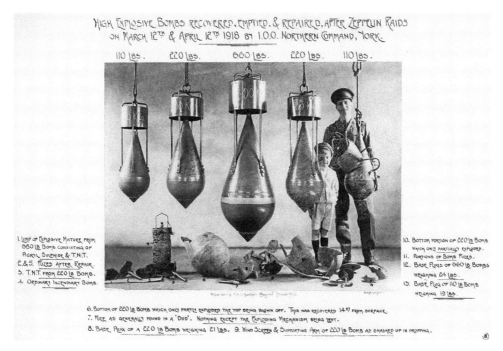

HIGH EXPLOSIVE BOMBS RECOVERED, EMPTIED, & REPAIRED, AFTER ZEPPELIN RAIDS ON MARCH 12TH & APRIL 12TH 1918 BY I.O.O. NORTHERN COMMAND, YORK.

110 lbs.   220 lbs.   660 lbs.   220 lbs.   110 lbs.

1. LUMP OF EXPLOSIVE MIXTURE FROM 660 lb BOMB CONSISTING OF PICRIL SULPHIDE & T.N.T.
2.&3. FUZES AFTER REPAIR.
3. T.N.T. FROM 220 lb BOMB.
4. ORDINARY INCENDIARY BOMB.

6. BOTTOM OF 220 lb BOMB WHICH ONLY PARTLY EXPLODED THE TOP BEING BLOWN OFF. THIS WAS RECOVERED 14 FT FROM SURFACE.
7. FUZE AS GENERALLY FOUND IN A 'DUD'. NOTHING EXCEPT THE EXPLODING MECHANISM BEING LEFT.
8. BASE PLUG OF A 220 lb BOMB WEIGHING 21 lbs. 9. WIND SCREEN & SUPPORTING ARM OF 220 lb BOMB AS SMASHED UP IN DROPPING.

10. BOTTOM PORTION OF 220 lb BOMB WHICH ONLY PARTIALLY EXPLODED.
11. PORTIONS OF BOMB FUZES.
12. BASE PLUGS OF 660 lb BOMBS WEIGHING 84 lbs.
13. BASE PLUG OF 110 lb BOMB WEIGHING 19 lbs.

Dud explosives and incendiary bombs. The percussion detonators for the incendiaries can be seen bottom left as 2 and 5. (IWM Q061163)

By December 1916, the north was protected by four full-strength squadrons of BE2cs with 69 landing strips from the Humber to the Forth. These were accompanied by observer posts all over the country, connected by telephone to warning control centres that directed the regional defences to the alert. Old artillery pieces were placed at various points on the north-eastern coast and towns that had been bombed. As the armies on the Western Front expanded, the desire for guns also increased depriving the defence systems of up-to-date pieces for a time and some areas had to use two old pounder guns that could not fire shells to any great altitudes. Eighteen-pounder guns gradually became the standard piece, although only towards the latter part of 1916 and early 1917. However, the need for men and machines elsewhere would sap the home defences of their strength.

By late 1918, the London Air Defence Area had been firmly established out of the haphazard and the almost patchwork mixture of operations beforehand. This created a standardised grid system of reporting for home defence units, which separated the zones for guns and aircraft. This was expanded for the rest of the country and led to the basis for defensive plans in the Second World War. It had been created by Maj.-Gen. EB Ashmore of the Royal Artillery.

At Stockton on Tees, there was a wireless direction finder, which could pick up the Zeppelins' message traffic and approximate the positions. Sound detection had been experimented with and was tried out with varying degrees of success.

Fixed concrete dishes or sound mirrors of 4 m high, constructed at various points on the east coast, focused on the sound waves of the engines of a distant raider into the headset of an officer, who could then notify the local home defence stations and the police, who would warn the local populations. Later developments of this method involved a moveable set of smaller acoustic mirrors, which could be located on high buildings and swivelled to track the intruder. In some cases, these sets were still in use with the military in the near and far east during the Second World War.

Other explanations for unexpected events at night were accounted for; groups of men heard marching through a village in the middle of the night materialised into a herd of cows that had escaped from a field, reports of lights in fields near Grantham in Lincolnshire appeared to be escaping marsh gas.

The arrest of two 'spies' at an Admiralty Telegraphic Station on the east coast turned out to be two men repairing the building.

Distrust and anxiety increased towards the new and unusual, as raids over Norfolk and London mounted, this began to prove the Zeppelins' sinister ability and invulnerability. In addition to the Defence of the Realm Act regulations, other physical attempts to hinder the unabated freedom over English skies fell flat, which caused contempt for the air force pilots who seemed incapable of bringing a raider down. The press fuelled rumours with emotive language, covering the anonymous raids locally, heightening suspicion of strangers in bombed areas with feelings that spies might have signalled to the enemy craft to bomb the area.

Throughout all of this, the British sense of humour always found material in the vein of seaside-type comic postcards and cartoons. Thousands of types were produced from the sentimental to the limits of Edwardian taste (for some). For example, there was a cartoon of a man shouting 'Take Cover' outside a ladies' public toilet and another of policemen discussing whether there's too much light coming from a house window where a silhouetted lady is evidently undressing preparing to go to bed.

French reaction to raids on France had been slightly different. Images of a Zeppelin over a child were published as post cards. In one, a child was thumbing its nose towards the airship, and another featured a child smoking a pipe looking up innocently as a Zeppelin loomed in the background!

It was reported that in Lincolnshire, in September 1916, two men were fined £1 each for striking a match after a Zeppelin warning had been given as well as fining another man the same amount for verbally abusing the policeman who knocked the lit cigarette from his hand. In the same police court proceedings, the Chief Constable complained at the conduct of young people after raid warnings were sounded, having paraded in the streets, singing and making noises; the threat was inferred that if this behaviour was repeated, there would be an application for the military to enforce a curfew after raid warnings, with any person breaching it ending up in court. In this place, unnamed in the report, stated that electric buzzers were sounded to signify a raid and that everyone should extinguish any lights.

I think I'm safe from Zepps here—they daren't spoil the boss's umbrella.

One of many humorous postcards produced.

Around the same time in Radcliffe near Bury, a number of men were fined 6s and woman 10s for breaching the Lighting Restrictions order with the evidence provided by three policemen.

To supplement the searchlights and guns, the home defence squadrons were filled with the most numerous home defence aircraft of this time, the BE2c.

This type would become a successful anti-Zeppelin aircraft, but simultaneously losses of these were high on the Western Front in daylight combat with other conventional aircraft.

Another early night fighter was the FE2b. A two-seat 'pusher' type with the engine and propeller behind the pilot and gunner, who had to stand in the exposed front cockpit to fire his Lewis gun – a perilous position if evasive manoeuvres were carried out.

Earlier aircraft types of 1914 had no armament, so the pilots used to fix lee Enfield service rifles or hunting guns to the side of cockpits, pointing away from the propeller arc. Other types were quickly developed, but many found they were quickly outclassed all too soon.

Up until 1917, the BE2c was usually the more frequently used type of aircraft until more powerful types became available such as DH4s, Sopwith Camels, Bristol Fighters and SE5as.

With no suitable ammunition immediately available there had been a variety of measures tried and found to be more dangerous to the RNAS pilots than the enemy. One of these was the testing of the *Le Prieur* rocket, as used on the Western Front. It was fitted into a tube on the aircrafts struts in containers – these were electrically fired but were sometimes found to not leave the tubes at all and on occasion explode while still on board the aircraft. Other early anti-Zeppelin

Believed to be the cockpit of modified RNAS Sopwith Pup 9905 regularly flown by Sub Lt Fane, equipped with a Lewis gun instead of the standard Vickers gun. (© Trustees of the National Museum of the Royal Navy)

attacks came in the form of aircraft trying to bomb them in mid-air with small cooper bombs or pierce the hydrogen bags with explosive 'Ranken' darts. There were attempts to use rifle grenades and Hale incendiary bombs – which had to be dropped directly on top of the target as Warneford had done.

This resulted in Zeppelins having machine gun platforms installed on their top sections and sometimes one gun on the stern. There was even the fiery grapnel, which was suspended beneath the aircraft supposedly hooking into an airship and igniting the hydrogen, it was apparently tested successfully with observation balloons but not in practice against raiders.

There was the Davis gun, which was a large recoilless gun invented by Cdr Davis of the US Navy in 1911. It was looked upon with interest but was only taken up with RNAS flying boats, which were big enough to carry for anti-submarine patrols. Eventually, the more optimistic/dangerous methods were quietly dropped, as the machine gun became the primary anti-Zeppelin weapon with the development of incendiary ammunition. This spelt the end of the Zeppelins' unrivalled indestructible liberty of the skies over England at night.

BE2cs had a Lewis gun pointed at a 45 degree angle in front of the pilot to fire through a gap in the top wing. So the aircraft could fly underneath, parallel to the

Zeppelin, and fire upwards instead of having to point the aircraft at the airship to fire. Some had Lewis guns mounted on a pintle in front of the cockpit to be able to change magazines without having to stand up to do it.

Although, this type of aircraft had suffered heavily over the Western Front during late 1915 and 1916, as the new Fokker aircraft had the advantage of speed over these slower types, it was suited to the slower, less manoeuvrable Zeppelins.

The home defence pilots were equally at risk from night sorties they were carrying out without the added danger of attempting to destroy a Zeppelin containing 1,130,000 cubic feet of hydrogen. There was the simple issue of reliability of aircraft and weaponry, open cockpits and hours of freezing temperatures while on patrol to contend. An additional frustration was that, in the days before radar was even dreamt of, many sorties were flown without ever sighting a raiding Zeppelin.

Using ordinary ammunition could only puncture the bags; if punctures occurred, the airships sail-maker would scale the inter-cell rope ladders of the ship to locate the damage and repair it. In L21's case, the aircraft would have had 18 gas cells to maintain.

Twin Lewis Guns on a French Nieuport 17. (© Trustees of the National Museum of the Royal Navy)

An Australian, Pomeroy, was supported by the Munitions Inventions Department in late 1915, and his invention of 1908 was found to be more effective than Brock's explosive bullet. Although initially volatile, by mid-1916 issues were cured going into full production along with the design by J. F. Buckingham of a phosphorous incendiary bullet, just in time for the new super 30s, the L30 class of Zeppelins to make their appearance.

> The bullet ... devised and perfected by Flight Lieutenant F. A. Brock show distinct promise in sinking Zeppelins ... The bullets will function at extreme ranges with velocity of about 100 ft. a second ... The result of the final unofficial trials by [the] Air Department, which took place on Monday, 14th February, was that the Lewis gun with ... about 20 inches of exhaust gases between the hydrogen ballonet and the air; fired the target at the 7th shot.
> Firing at a range of 600 Yards, on 5 fabric targets in a high wind very good practice was made, and all the bullets except one exploded in passing the 3rd target, the majority in the 2nd or 3rd, or between these two screens ... these bullets have been proved of some considerable use against heavier than machines; alas one bullet will cause enough damage to the main spar or inter-plane strut to bring about the destruction of the machine.

It was a commonly held, but mistaken, belief among the British that within the airships the Germans pumped engine exhaust gases around the gas bags to neutralise any hits that would have otherwise ignited the hydrogen. As the report shows, the test included this technique and, even with it, succeeded in igniting the ballonet.

The bullets were initially loaded onto ammunition belts wholly as one type; later pilots and gunners were instructed to alternate a variety of bullet types. For example, Brock–Tracer–Buckingham–Brock–Tracer–Buckingham. The ammunition would make up the 250 round belts on Vickers, and 40 and 90 round drum magazines on Lewis guns. This was taken on by front-line RFC units in the last two years of the war. The report states that the bullets were safe if a blockage or misfire happened – this has been disputed by other first-hand accounts. Once the bullets had come into regular use, other more adventurous anti-airship methods were quietly dropped and consigned to history.

The losses for the German Airship Service came all at once, starting with *Hauptmann* Schramm's SL11, a Schutte-Lanz a laminated wood-framed airship shot down by RFC pilot Leefe-Robinson on 3 September, flying a BE2c using the new ammunition.

SL11 was incinerated totally to ash with the metal components distorted and melted in the midst of it, along with the crew reduced to roasted entangled forms with stumps and exposed skulls that the onlookers could hardly believe that a few hours earlier to be real human beings. It was felt by some in the higher echelons of the British command that the public would not understand the differences between a Schutte-Lanz and a Zeppelin with all references to the raiders totally referring

One postcard of a series of the end of SL11 taken by H. Scott Orr from the top of a house in Woodford Green, Essex.

Sanctioned by Official Press Bureau.   **NEARING THE END.**   Copyright. H. Scott Orr.
About 2-22 a.m. Sunday, Sept. 3rd, 1916.

to the Zeppelins in one form or other in the public domain. The SL11 wreck was labelled the L21 in the news, photographs and in mementos salvaged from the wreck – a mistaken identity that still persist to this day.

The day before the Lancashire raid, a huge Zeppelin effort had concentrated on the southern and eastern counties. This mass attack came as it was proven that SL11's demise had been no fluke. The newest types went down – one of the first kill of two Zeppelins with the L32 (Werner Petersen) – on 24 September, burned in Essex to RFC pilot Sowrey. And L33 (Alois Bocker) crash-landed with the crew being arrested by a local constable near Little Wigborough.

On 1 October, under the command of Heinrich Mathy, L31 fell to the guns of 2nd Lt Tempest over Potters Bar. Mathy jumped as his ship fell and survived just long enough for the onlookers to find him alive and for him to be aware of his surroundings.

Within four weeks, the airship service had been shaken to its core; things would never be the same again. In November 1916, the second kill of two Zeppelins in one night later proved beyond all reasonable doubt that their combat days were numbered, not least so shocking that it was the most experienced raiding crews that had gone down.

Pitt Klein was a former petty officer on a Zeppelin:

Our nerves are ruined by mistreatment. If anyone should say that he was not haunted by visions of burning airships, when he would be a braggart. But nobody makes this assertion; everyone has the courage to confess his dreams and thoughts.

Stereoscopic card of the wreck of L33.

CHAPTER 5

L 21

L21 was built at Löwenthal in Fredrichshafen on the shores of Lake Constance in the southern Baden-Württemberg region of Germany.

Commissioned on 10 January 1916, under the command of Max Dietrich, L21 started operational life housed in the *Norbert* shed at Nordholz in northern Germany.

Its hydrogen volume was calculated as 1,264,100 square feet, contained within 18 gas cells. During its short life of 10 months, it carried out 17 scouting flights and 10 raids.

The power came from four Maybach HSLu engines of 240 hp each. These were housed in the control (1) and after-gondola (3); resulting in the total power output of 960 hp.

L21 (LZ61) Q Class Specification

- 179 m in length
- 18.9 m in diameter
- Four 240 hp Maybach engines (hp – horsepower tuned to mode of propeller)

L21 in January 1916 at Nordholz, near Bremenhaven, Northern Germany. (© Aeronauticum Luftschiffe Nordholz)

L21's second commander
Hauptman August Stelling
and crew next to the
Command Gondola.
(© Aeronauticum Luftschiffe
Nordholz)

- Maximum speed of 58 mph
- Maximum range – 3,000 miles
- Service ceiling of 11,500 feet
- Payload of 38,800 Ibs
- Empty weight calculated at 52,950 Ibs
- Based at Nordholz on commissioning
- Seddin from 21 February 1916 – Out of action for six weeks due to nose being crushed on hanger door.
- Tondern from 5 April 1916
- Nordholz from 16 April 1916

Flights: (4 factory; 17 scouting; 10 completed raids)
Raids dropping 14,442 kg bombs
- 31 January 1916 – Midlands
- 24–25 April 1916
- 2–3 May 1916
- 28–29 July 1916
- 2–3 August 1916
- 8–9 August 1916
- 2–3 September 1916 – Norfolk
- 23–24 September 1916 – Suffolk
- 25–26 September 1916 – Lancashire
- 1–2 October 1916 – Midlands
- 27–28 November 1916 – Destroyed

Kurt Frankenberg took command on 15 August 1916 from its second commander
August Stelling, whose short tenure of command since 24 June ended. L21 had
been returned to the Nobel shed at Nordholz from Tondern's Toska shed.

Frankenberg, an experienced Zeppelin officer having been with Bocker on the L5 and L14, had been set to take command of L33 but was ordered to take command of L21 instead, with a new crew made up mostly of newly trained men with a few old hands among them. The second in command was *Leutnant zur See* (*LzS*) Hans-Werner Salzbrunn, a young officer from Berlin, who after passing the endurance tests was posted to L21.

On 2/3 September 1916, L21 dropped bombs in the grounds of the royal residence at Sandringham in Norfolk, no damage was reported on the ground; although, the Sandringham AA gun did claim a hit on the Zeppelin. If the Kaiser had known, it surely would have been the end of Frankenberg's Zeppelin career; yet, he reported, he had bombed Norwich.

On L21, the bombsight operator was *LzS* Hans-Werner Salzbrunn; the Carl Zeiss bombsights were situated at the front of the control gondola, along with the bomb release switches.

He would have made a bombsight setting on the airship's altitude from the altimeter then measuring the speed over the ground by using a stopwatch to measure the distance between two points through the crosshairs of the bombsight, hypothetically measuring a space of 300 m between the two points. Zeppelin altimeters were actually aneroid barometers displaying air pressure scaled to read in meters.

Not long after L21s attack on Bolton, on 1 October, while heading inland from the west Norfolk area over central England, the crews of L21 and other raiders

Frankenberg's crew of L21 and company. (© Aeronauticum Luftschiffe Nordholz)

that night witnessed, many miles to the south, a Zeppelin caught in the London searchlights in flames, slowly falling to earth, glowing in the evening sky.

It had been L31, the ship of the most experienced Zeppelin commander Heinrich Mathy, whose death caused shockwaves in Germany.

Name	Rank	Date of Birth	Place of Birth	Date of Death
Alfred Brieger	Ob.Masch.Mt.	04.03.1889	Kohlfurt	28.11.1916
Albert Carlsen	Ob.Sig.Mt.	06.10.1888	Neumünster	28.11.1916
Kurt Frankenberg	Oblt z S	30.04.1887	Kassel	28.11.1916
Otto Gras	Ob.Btsmt.	20.03.1888	Delitzsch	28.11.1916
Hans Hintzer	Ob.Masch.Mt.	17.01.1886	Culmisch	28.11.1916
Christian Jensen	Steurmann	26.03.1883	Amrum	28.11.1916
Theophil Kaczikowski	Ob.Matr.	30.04.1890	Zuckau	28.11.1916
Wichl Kiel	Ob.Masch.Mt.	01.12.1884	Elende	28.11.1916
Walter Klann	Masch.Mt.	07.10.1880	Elbing	28.11.1916
Wilhelm Mezger	Ob.Matr.	25.05.1893	Tuttlingen	28.11.1916
Paul Petznik	FT-Mt.	12.09.1889	Bromberg	28.11.1916
Otto Prinke	Sig.Mt.	22.07.1888	Wrist	28.11.1916
Anton Reischel	Masch.	05.03.1882	Dresden	28.11.1916
Hans-Werner Salzbrunn	OlzS	21.12.1892	Berlin	28.11.1916
Theodor Schmidt	Ob.Masch.Mt.	30.09.1887	Danzig	28.11.1916
Alfred Schwarz	Masch.Mt.	15.03.1891	Rostock i.M.	28.11.1916
Wilhelm Wittkugel	Btsmt.d.R.	18.01.1890	Stadthagen	28.11.1916 [37]

CHAPTER 6

THE LANCASHIRE RAID, 25–26 SEPTEMBER

Target: London & the Industrial Midlands
Zeppelins: L14, L16, L21, L22, L23, L30, L31

Weather: Gales and rain had precipitated the arrival of an anti-cyclonic depression, travelling across from the Atlantic, passing over to the North Sea, over the course of the week. The weather across England was perfect for the raid, still and clear with patchy cloud, as it was on the eastern side of the North Sea, conditions were perfect and again the Zeppelins set off, to the wondering gaze of many ground crew below – rising from their bases and in a short while disappearing into the distance.

L21's Route on 25–26 September, 1916

Nordholz–Sutton on Sea–Sheffield–Derwent–Todmorden–Lumb–Newchurch–Ewood Bridge–Ramsbottom–Holcombe–Holcombe Brook–Bolton–Blackburn–Burnley–Bolton Abbey–Whitby–Nordholz

On the 25 September, on the Western Front, British and New Zealand troops achieved success in the Battle of Morval, part of the Flers-Courcelette struggle during the Somme offensive.

While on the British mainland, life continued in the accepted manner brought about by wartime. The casualty lists and mourning of those lost in distant battles was a constant factor of life. In some streets, the whole populace was in mourning for friends or family, while changes went on. Factories all over the country turned out war material, thousands of women were employed in a plethora of new roles unthinkable before the war, from manning the thousands of auxiliary hospitals up and down the country to becoming welders, blacksmiths, ammunition workers, mechanics, fitters and forestry workers. Thousands were working overtime and night shifts. Children still went to school, many with the awareness of their fathers' and brothers' absence from their lives and the uncertainty of their situation; life for many went on as normal – the routines of hard working people at home went on whether in office or mill, field or ship.

For able-bodied seaman Joseph Murray of the Royal Naval Division, 25 September was the last day of his first leave since returning from Gallipoli and he had squeezed into a carriage of a night train en route from Edinburgh to Newcastle., sitting on his pack in a corner. The train was packed with troops returning to the front and the conversations around him were of the two Zeppelins shot down the previous night, many were reading papers of the spectacles in the south. There had been much speculation as to the new theories that sparks from the funnels of steam trains all over the country were leading the raiders to targets.

On the other side of the North Sea, the Imperial Naval Airship Service was taking advantage of the continuing good weather, issuing orders to raid industrial middle England, though with caution. With the bomb sites of the previous night being searched for survivors and the burned skeletal wrecks of the L32 and L33 hardly cooled, Frankenberg and his scarcely rested crew were on board L21, to go about their duty once more over the North Sea heading for the English coast – undoubtedly with the awareness of what had happened to the brand new 'Super 30s'.

Part of a raiding force consisting of seven Zeppelins, they followed the coast from Nordholz down off Holland and headed due west for Norfolk, where they used lighthouses along the Norfolk coast as landmarks and from there accurately judged their positions.

L21 is recorded as having crossed the English coast at Sutton on Sea in Lincolnshire at approximately 9.45 p.m., 40 minutes ahead of L22.

L21 over Nordholz. (© Aeronauticum Luftschiffe Nordholz)

Postcard of Sutton on Sea.

At 10.30 p.m., L21 passed over Lincoln, bypassing Bawtry at 10.55 p.m., reaching the northern proximity of Sheffield at about 11.08 p.m.

Air-raid warnings had sounded, but active organisation was poor, as the AA officers were enjoying the pleasures of the home front, attending a ball. Capt. Edward Clifton of the RFC took off in his BE2c from Coal Aston airfield. Due to poor visibility, he could not locate L21 and crash-landed, fortunately escaping injury; unfortunately, then being unable to seek out L22 that did bomb the city.

Frankenberg flew north avoiding Sheffield, which unlike Bolton had searchlights and several anti-aircraft guns. At some point, heading away from Sheffield and certainly having navigational problems, L21 steered north-west over the black undulating landscape of the Peak District, passing Oldham to the west and Huddersfield to the east. L21 was reported at Derwent at 11.28 p.m. before disappearing from observers and, on chancing upon a train bound for Manchester via Todmorden where the locomotive stopped, was sighted there at 11.55 p.m., but the Zeppelin continued on over the darkened hills past Bacup.

Rossendale

The noise of the engines was heard at 11.50 p.m., and L21 was visible near Bacup at 11.55 p.m., heading over Lancashire; the police recorded that a hostile airship had passed over the borough during the night without dropping any bombs. This was fortunate for both the workers and residents, and even more so as here there were two national shell factories: one at Irwell Mill, producing 4.5-inch ammunition, and another at Height Barn Mill.

Now they were over the industrialised county of Lancashire, which in 1912–13 produced three-quarters of the world's cotton goods and was now manufacturing a plethora of war material. Despite this, they were truly unprepared for any kind of enemy air attack.

This was a clear night with stars shining clearly above, the stillness of the night. The quiet, occasionally interrupted by the occasional owl screech or the rustling of branches caught by a breeze, was about to be punctuated with the unexpected distant humming of engines overhead.

A police constable on his beat witnessed the Zeppelin seeming to be almost stationary shortly before the bombardment. This may have been due to the wireless operator receiving a wave co-ordinates signal and the preparation of crew to bombing positions.

On the hillside above the village of Lumb to the north of Waterfoot and Cloughfold, an incendiary was released hitting near Field Top farm causing no damage, then within eight minutes there had reportedly been another 12 or 15 bombs dropped, as L21 droned away over the Rawtenstall area.

The diary of Mr J. H. Whipp, a long-term manager at the Grime bridge colliery, records that 'the Zeppelin passed over the Co [sic] factory at Lumb at 12.05 and dropped an incendiary at Field top farm, next on to Rawtenstall dropping several bombs, blowing windows out but no lives lost'. He also states that Ewood Bridge station had been completely destroyed in addition to great destruction en route there were apparently 30 to 40 lives lost in Bury and Bolton.

This embroidering may well be due to the speculative nature of Chinese whispers and exaggerations that flourished in a time when news was not instantly available but in dribs and drabs through gossip, supposition and later on carefully censored newspapers. As in incidents today on the television news, the internet or in print, there is always debate about casualties, damage and what may have occurred through the prism of facts known at that moment – which are usually short on actual detail and accuracy due to the immediacy of events.

Frankenberg headed away from Lumb at speed, south-west over Seat Naze, where another incendiary was released – failing to go off near Height Side House . It is on permanent display at Whittaker Park museum in Rawtenstall. Apparently, it was taken by tram to the police station by a special constable.

The witnesses to this were most likely alerted by the explosions as well as the noise of the engines, which has been reported on as appearing as a distinctive whining 'woom-woom-woom' sound. Many hundreds of people gravitated out onto the pavements and roads to catch glimpse of the Zepp.

Here it would have passed near to Waterfoot, seen and heard by the family and friends of Stoker Alexander Logan, who was killed on board flagship HMS Lion at the battle of Jutland.

Then over Lea Bank Hall, another bomb fell into the adjoining field near to Fall Barn. This was close to one HMWCM (His Majesties Waste Cotton Mills) at

The failed Goldschmidt incendiary at Whitaker Park complete with slightly singed labels and streamer. (© Scott Carter-Clavell)

Cloughfold Cotton Cellulose Works, 'the rag shop', which was firing up the boilers for the day's production of cotton.

Part of this bomb was found on the driveway of the hall, the then home of Col Craven Hoyle. The bomb was fenced off and detonated by soldiers on the following Saturday. When the bomb exploded, the tons of soil that had been packed on top was hurled into the air.

The colonel later alluded to the raid in his speech for the opening of the 25-bed Kitchener ward at Newhallhey military hospital, which had been funded through

The detonation. A photo taken by John Hirst. Lea Bank Hall is to the left of the photo. (© Rawtenstall Library)

his personal generosity. In his speech, he stated that the people in the raided areas now knew the possible horrors of war. The 'disagreeable greetings cards' left by the raider should make towns that escaped casualties feel thankful for their providential escape and show their appreciation in a substantial manner.

A writer for the Rossendale free press in the 1960s recalled seeing the Zeppelin, after being hurriedly dressed and taken outside as a four-year-old to see the silver cigar-shaped object 'sailing awesomely yet majestically' over Cribden Hill, and later on that week seeing the craters in fields near Ewood Bridge. This witness must have viewed this from a north-westerly direction making the airship seem like it was over Cribden Hill (above the ski centre) where in fact the Zeppelin was travelling over the Newchurch/Cloughfold area before heading to the bridge.

Heading over Cloughfold station to the south-west, L21's next bomb fell on Hall Carr Road near a farm creating, a hole that is said by William Capell to be able to accommodate a horse and cart.

Whinberry Naze escaped unscathed, as L21 continued west towards Irwell Vale, attracting the curious gaze of thousands below. One lady went outside her house to see why there was so much talking at this early hour – returning inside, she roused some of her family with the news of the Zeppelin to be told by her uncle that 'ne'er heed up, we might as weel die in bed as ony where' (Never, head up, we might as well die in bed as anywhere).

Despite the numerous and tremendous explosions and concussions in the Rossendale valley that night, the much vaunted *Zepp* attracted more curiosity than actual panic. These were the people who they were at war with. Those that everyone was all too aware of, the baby killers, the faceless enemies whose actions had caused the all too constant changes in their lives, the economy, industry and by association thousands of workers had been geared to defeat this as yet unseen force. Yet, they're here over Rossendale paying a fleeting visit.

The *Bury Guardian* reported on 27 September in reference to the area with much anonymity that the peaceful slumbers of town-dwellers were disturbed by bangs. The article stating the engine's 'whirr' had been heard much earlier, then subsequently the thunderous booms of bombs, with slight property damage and no casualties reported.

Rawtenstall fortunately escaped the attentions of the Zeppelin.

Hundreds of people were reported to be out on the darkened streets staring upwards watching the events unfold. As L21 was turning over the golf course, two bombs, an explosive and incendiary, were dropped. A lady had appeared out of the Bridge End Hotel on Helmshore road to watch the *Zepp*, but her attire drew consternation from the collected crowd who thought the whiteness of her apron would attract the raider and urged her back inside!

These bombs fell onto what are now the playing fields of Haslingden High School off Green Lane and the incendiary onto the golf course. The crater near the golf course became an attraction in the following days.

It was reported that the bombs could actually be seen falling from the Zeppelin by the lights of the fuses burning or the simple innocence on the part of the

New Hall Hey Mills early twentieth century. (By kind permission of Ramsbottom Heritage Society)

observers that this most likely was the reflection upon the surface of the explosive bomb casings as they fell – as explosives were armed by a small propeller and the incendiaries were ignited by impact on the percussion fuses on hitting the ground.

The Rossendale free press report praised the conduct of the population in that, as unaccustomed as they were to Zeppelins, unlike the east coast the area, 'had stood the experience quietly and well'.

The *Haslingden Gazette* later reported that 'people behaved with remarkable calmness and centred their attention on tracing the cigar shaped murder craft in the sky'.

The first target of a semi-industrial nature to be hit was the water works between Ewood Bridge and Irwell Vale. At this point the treatment ponds may have appeared as holding tanks for industrial use.

Four bombs hit in and around the facility, whereas two fell a little further on damaging the track of the East Lancashire Railway, a total of nine having been dropped, three failed to detonate. Reportedly, the bombs that detonated fell into soft earth leaving craters 6 yards wide.

An explosive had fallen 30-odd yards away from cottages at Irwell Vale and shattered the doors and windows, but caused no injuries. Here a 10-inch telegraph pole was split by a huge shrapnel splinter and a stone wall was shattered by the blast. Shrapnel marks can still be seen on the houses, most notably near the bridge at the Hardsough Lane end.

By 2.45 a.m. in the Rossendale area, the situation was reported to be normal again, during the raid it appears that the electricity supply was cut off but was restored at this time. Incidentally, the area had received electricity in 1911, in 1916 there were 297 customers using 399 kilowatts in 850,000 units. Supply was usually linked to installation of electrified tramway wires.

In the morning, a farmer and his family nearby at Cockham were discovered to have slept on mattresses dragged from the farmhouse to a field, which they had considered a safer place to be out in the open!

One witness, on the day after, told a journalist that he saw a boy carrying a heavy cylindrical black object (incendiary bomb), which evidently had not gone

Irwell Vale & Mill
– the cottages can
be seen centre left.
(© Bury Archives)

Shrapnel marks can still
be seen on the end row
at Irwell Vale. (© Scott
Carter-Clavell)

off, and he and a friend had pulled it from the earth and, oblivious to the risk, were taking it to the nearest policeman's house!

Over Rossendale, L21 was reported to be travelling fairly quickly across the sky, as it was reported past Helmshore and headed down the valley, probably following the East Lancashire Railway lines to their port side; Frankenberg was over the Stubbins and Ramsbottom area. It was, probably, around this point, if not earlier, high up in the control gondola that someone spotted a dull glow in the distance.

In the Helmshore area, some residents had believed the area too far inland to be troubled by air raids. One resident stated thagt they had experienced Germanic frightfulness and desired no more!

Unlike southern and eastern neighbourhoods, the northern populations' main exposure to the Zeppelin had been through the press and word-of-mouth, stories of the 'baby killers' travelling far and wide. The inquisitive reactions of the people on this night observing L21 from below, under the circumstances, is understandable;

much like crowds gathering for an albeit less sinister and destructive Royal visit to a town or the massive attention the Tour de France routes through Yorkshire received in 2014 – a once in a lifetime chance to see the much publicised famous visitors on home turf. Indeed, the Zeppelin's visit to Bolton certainly drew bigger crowds than the King's visit in 1913.

Ramsbottom and Holcombe

L21 came south down the Rossendale valley over the Ramsbottom area continuing to drop more bombs.

The exact sequence of this attack is not clear, but I have plotted an approximate course over the known and approximated positions of the bombs. It is worth remembering, though, the actual raid occurred very quickly; L21 did not linger over the area but kept going. At altitude and varying speeds, the bombs released seem to have landed without any sense of a definitive target.

Coming southward, high over the valley, two explosive bombs fell into the field between the Rake and Victoria Street, now a residential area.

Near the Rake, an explosive landed in the driveway of Woodside off Dundee Lane, very quickly followed by the four explosives detonating in Holcombe village.

As these exploded, L21 was already turning southward, dropping two explosives that cratered the field a distance behind the butcher's shop at 28 Bolton Road West.

Another then dropped onto Giles Taylors Mineral Water Works in Regent Street, succeeded by an incendiary into a field at Lumb Carr Farm. This was followed by an incendiary into a cottage at Pot Green Holcombe Brook.

These, where possible, will be detailed in the following pages.

Ramsbottom seen from Helmshore Road, 1900. (By kind permission of Ramsbottom Heritage Society)

A journalist staying on the outskirts of Ramsbottom reported on hearing the attack,

> It was not exactly a bang but a bung repeated four times in quick succession causing a violent vibration of the air with a whirlpool effect. It was a weird experience. The suggesting they were closer than they actually were. The atmospheric currents evidently taking fantastic courses.

Though various somewhat unreliable press accounts give different facts and figures, the number of bombs ranged from three to nine in the whole assault on this area. The official General Headquarters (GHQ) report lists seven high explosives in and around Holcombe and Ramsbottom.

A 14-year-old boy living in Callender Street was awakened by what he thought was the clattering of the night-soil men with their Shire horse and cart upon the cobbles. As his father and brother took him outside to see the true reason for the noise, the distant form of a Zeppelin could be seen. He said that nothing like this was expected yet there was no panic but rumours abounded that the raider was following a train to Manchester.

Night-soil or honey-pot men would collect human faeces from the non-flushing back yard toilets of terraced houses and spread it on the fields as fertilizer.

Holcombe

The crew of L21 followed the railway lines from Ewood Bridge at an undetermined altitude but possibly at about 5,000 feet. As they approached the Ramsbottom area, it's quite possible that they found that the features of the ground gradually became indistinguishable.

Holcombe village school, 1906.
(© Bury Archives)

Every residence would have had at least one coal fire with the closely built nature of works and houses. Cotton mills, foundries, bleach works and paper mills each with their own boilers, chimneys and steam engines sat by the rows of terraces in Ramsbottom. For instance, on the 1910 Ordnance Survey Map, there were approximately 26 industrial chimneys of various types in the town, the majority of these concentrated along the bottom of the valley close to the railway with its large sidings; north of the station would have been a very active hub. This means there would have been quite a smoky atmosphere hanging in the still night air between the town and the Zeppelin.

This in itself would have hugely reduced the visibility for the crew, not to mention the fact that the buildings themselves were darkened by years of soot, so together this reduction of visibility – even to the point where street lights still lit and houses showing lights were masked by hanging smoke. The calm and still *Zepp night* weather worked well for the residents of Ramsbottom, but Holcombe, sitting higher up on the hillside, must have either been visible above the smog or unthinking lighting was showing.

Any sudden or repeated display of light would render the un-careful a certain target, there had been cases where bombings happened on small villages – whereas in the cities people were more aware of blackout restrictions.

Those residents still awake may have been showing lights, flickering of candles, a gas lamp burning bright or perhaps the glare from a fire however dim against the darkened landscape would have clearly revealed to those searching eyes up in the gondolas that there was something alive down there. Given that blackout controls were not strictly enforced in this area, as air raids were not deemed a serious enough threat – the general feeling was Zeppelins were not a threat this far inland.

Many villagers in bed were unaware of anything unusual happening; however, some residents were aware of the emanation of strange noises from the valley, which were likened by more than one person to thunder and railway noises – engines shunting and fog signals. A few looked out in curiosity into the darkness. It was remarked upon that there had been no warning of the raid, as the first many knew of it was the explosions outside. One villager said to live near the church stated on evacuating his wife and child that the raid was over in a very few minutes.

Two bombs fell on either side of the school; the first demolishing on the east side the corner of the stone wall, peppering the wall of the school with shrapnel and shattering the windows; though, internally there was not too much destruction, a partition was smashed but pictures and gas globes were intact. The cellar window here had been blown in and a nut severed from a safety valve on the heating system. The concussion of this bomb stopped the church clock, as it was deflected down the side of the house opposite. In the days of gas lighting, buildings using naked flame from gas lamps or pendants – glass globes or shades were fitted to diffuse the light.

The blast of the second and third bomb on the west side of the school smashed the windows and frames of the row of cottages on Holcombe Road facing the school building. The explosions cratered the field of Higher Barn behind the school building and knocked over 15 feet of stone wall on Moor Road. The field craters were describedas being 18 feet in diameter.

Another bomb fell onto the road in front of what is now the Shoulder of Mutton pub car park and the opposite the Post Office. This crater was reported as being 8-feet deep and 12-feet wide; the displaced earth thrown 200–300 yards away. The shattered remnants of the shell casing in the crater was found by a resident, who took it as a trophy.

The postmaster and postmistress, Mr and Mrs Hoyle, and their sons were in bed. Mr Hoyle, who had been alerted to the noises from up the valley, had been in and out of bed peering through the venetian blind to see the cause of the disturbance.

Looking out again he saw a bright light falling, followed by a tremendous explosion directly in front of the building causing havoc within. Ceiling plaster fell, windows were smashed inwards by the blast, furniture shredded. In the Post Office downstairs, the vestibule had been shattered to matchwood, furniture was ruined. A clock on a sideboard had been catapulted on to a centre table, whereas a mirror on a side wall miraculously remained unbroken. The only human casualty in Holcombe was his wife Elizabeth, who suffered a cut to the back of her head from flying glass. Those who weren't so lucky were a thrush and a coop of chickens behind the school that took the brunt of a blast and were strewn across the field.

The school wall and collapsed stone wall corner. (By kind permission of Ramsbottom Heritage Society)

The crater was in the foreground of the photo and the old Post Office on the right of the image still bears a multitude of scars, which are plain to see on the front the building, now a private residence.

The front of the old Post Office building still bears the pockmarks of the bomb blast most clearly on the lintels. All the windows of the surrounding buildings were blown out – some with their frames. The pub lost its front door and 20 windows were broken. Some villagers realising what had befallen the village took the very sensible precaution of sheltering in the pub's cellar. Others rushed in their nightclothes to the sites of the explosions to see for themselves. Much excitement was reported among the villagers and witnesses, with fear being overridden by curiosity.

Though witnesses claim that they saw small beams of lights coming from the sky at the same time that the streaks of light said to be the fizzing fuses of bombs descending. This was probably imagination or naïve understanding of the modern explosive!

A special constable living in or near the village was interviewed afterwards by a press correspondent stating that he saw the Zeppelin with a neighbour who had been awakened after hearing what sounded like banging on a door and louder

The unfortunate thrush – now a registered war memorial. (© Scott Carter-Clavell)

explosion. To him the Zeppelin looked 10 yards long and at its great height the underside glistened almost white. He described a light slowly descending from the Zeppelin flaring like a 'Monstrous Bulls eye' illuminating the countryside beneath.

This account seems to suggest that they did drop a parachute flare. This witness also refers to the Zeppelin having circled over the area; though, I have not found any other evidence to suggest this happened, as the eyewitnesses to the initial explosions surely would have heard the raider pass by again, even if they hadn't seen it again. L21 certainly wasn't lingering but heading onwards quickly.

Described by a standardised press report in local papers after the raid as a village known for its rustic charms and frequented by Saturday picnic parties 'as being the object of German "frightfulness"'.

Peter Strasser, head of naval airships, had previously written to his mother: 'If what we do is frightful, then may frightfulness be Germany's salvation.'

After the raid, it was stated in the *Ramsbottom Observer* that the raid had occupied a very few minutes. Police, special constables and the fire brigade arrived in the village shortly after the raid, albeit with little they could do until morning, hunts for parts of the bombs turned up fragments that ended up in the hands of the police.

In the following days, word spread and thousands of people visited Holcombe to see for themselves what had happened. It was reported that the villagers referred to their experience with smiles, as the German visitors had expended a considerable quantity of ammunition for no other purpose than to provide a spell of excitement. The road crater was filled in shortly afterwards, as it was blocking the road and telegraph wires that had been brought down were repaired.

After the first bombs, L21 headed south-west and released explosives over the fields behind Bolton Road West – it was said that those craters remained there for many years marked by a pole. It may have been here that it was seen by the special constable in Holcombe, possibly dropping a parachute flare as well.

Frankenberg's next bomb fell onto a mineral water works on Regent Street, causing considerable destruction. The works owned by a Mr Giles Taylor was situated in some cottages recently converted into a factory.

Dwellings in Holcombe on Lumb Carr Road with Cross Lane and Peel Tower behind.

View from the hill into Holcombe 1936, the school can be seen in the centre. (By kind permission of Ramsbottom Heritage Society)

Here a large crater was made at the back, catapulting a joist from the building over it and into the opposite field – the explosion struck two motor lorries waiting to be loaded – badly damaging them and covering the area in a very fine dust, in addition to the numerous bottles, stoppers and corks strewn about.

Incredibly, nobody was injured or killed – all the more remarkable as nearby dwellings suffered many broken windows.

A field at Lumb Carr Farm between Bolton Road West and Lumb Carr Road was subjected to an incendiary, which didn't do much damage as the next did.

A Giles Taylor bottle. (© Scott Carter-Clavell)

Lumb Carr Farm. (By kind permission of Ramsbottom Heritage Society)

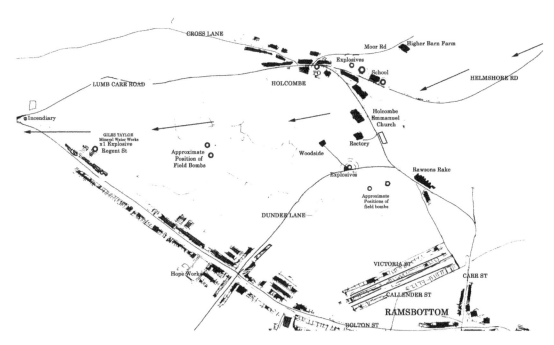

Map I

Holcombe Brook

At Holcombe Brook there were plenty of targets, the railway station and line to Bury or the three mills, which stood either side of the junction, there was Bank Mill and New York Mill opposite the Hare and Hounds and behind the pub was another cotton mill. Whatever the target was, an incendiary hit a house at Pot Green on Summerseat Lane just off the junction, going straight through the roof. As this was situated directly in front of Bank Mill, there may have been a light showing from the Mill, which highlighted the location.

The account was relayed in the following days by the press.

In a house at Holcombe Brook, two little girls aged six and three sleeping in one bedroom escaped injury, when an incendiary device crashed into their room. The father related an account to the journalists while still covered in the marks and discolouration of his mad dash through the flames to save his daughters.

> My wife, baby and I were asleep in the front bedroom, sometime after midnight I heard a startling boom from a field nearby. I rushed to the window, but before I had properly grasped what was happening there was another terrific report much nearer and more terrifying … there were flames bursting from the room in which our two little girls were sleeping. I knew nothing for the next two or three seconds. It was just a mad dash into the room … confused perception that the children were unhurt … then I was outside, feeling scorched and stifled, with one child in each arm. The elder one ask wonderingly what had made the room catch fire, the little one was still dozing …
>
> My wife and I were just wild with delight at their safety, and noticed nothing of the rest of the air raid.

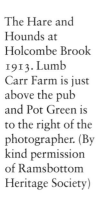

The Hare and Hounds at Holcombe Brook 1913. Lumb Carr Farm is just above the pub and Pot Green is to the right of the photographer. (By kind permission of Ramsbottom Heritage Society)

The bomb had actually crashed through the roof and then through the girls' bedroom floor, a yard from their bed, into the dining room below, leaving an oval hole in their floor. Neighbours rushed to their aid, the fire was extinguished and the house saved; it still stands today.

Nearby, the wounded French and Belgian soldiers convalescing at Hollymount convent at Greenmount would have, no doubt, been awakened by the sound of German military intrusion once more, as L21 droned by.

L21 was reported to be visible from Bury at 12.19 a.m.

Turning for the distant glow, Frankenberg passed across Two Brooks Valley between Hawkshaw and Affetside. Prior to this no human deaths had been caused by the raid; however, the first human casualty of the visit was an elderly resident of Turton Road. At Old Bates Farm grandmother Elizabeth Cranshaw succumbed to shock on sighting the Zeppelin high above Holcombe from Turton Road.

To the older generations brought up in the nineteenth century, the vision of the nation's sworn enemy traversing the heart of the Empire in the dead of night in huge silver cigar-shaped flying machines must have been mesmerising and terrifying in equal measure, surely posing many a pondered question as to what the future held.

The cessation of peaceful isolation in wartime so familiar to towns and cities in the south and east had befallen the residents of the Rossendale valley and was to abruptly wake thousands of slumbering Boltonians, as the hum of L21's four Maybach engines rhythmic 'whirr' gradually interrupted the freezing midnight stillness.

Now heading straight for Bolton down over Two Brooks Valley. They passed the firing ranges at Holcombe Moor and over the large two brooks bleach-works – no known bombs were dropped on this path as L21 travelled along the valley parallel to Turton Road, passing over Bradshaw Road, passing over Bromley Cross then Astley Bridge.

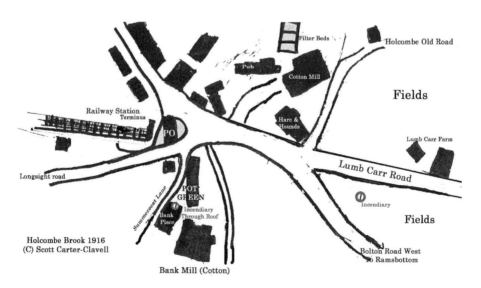

Map **2**

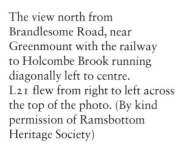

The view north from Brandlesome Road, near Greenmount with the railway to Holcombe Brook running diagonally left to centre. L21 flew from right to left across the top of the photo. (By kind permission of Ramsbottom Heritage Society)

Looking down from the freezing gondolas, the crew going about their tasks, lookouts leaning on their Spandau MG08s, scanning the unfamiliar dark hazy patchwork landscape below to the horizon gradually blending with the darkness. The dull glow southward, the glare from the furnaces was getting nearer, a beacon in the darkness.

This hadn't escaped the notice of the people below either.

Bolton

Many in the town had retired for the night, many were still very much awake. Some sat by their fires after a day's work and others on night shifts were going about their work in mills and foundries, a constant energy of production beneath the night sky. The vibrations from steam hammers crashing onto metal could be felt in the ground around the works, as could distant thudding. One of these can be seen next to College Way on the site of John Street. Glows from the molten metal shone out of windows, skylights and doorways. As well as the boiler houses of the mills threw out the occasional flash of light, as boilers doors were opened illuminating the dark with the intense blooms of warm light from the various mills. Gas street lamps were still lit. The residents of the many dark rows of terraced houses around the town were unaware of what was about to happen.

The skies were clear over Bolton when, from the north-east, L21 crossed the sky, noted by a solicitor as passing across the Milky Way. There is confusion over times with accounts frequently contradicting each other, it is reasonable to believe that times being approximated to whenever a contributor sighted L21.

Word of the visitor had reached Bessemers ironworks and workers were shutting the furnace doors, trying to stop the glow from the molten metal casting the beacon up into the sky. Their strenuous efforts evidently paid off as the area of Great Moor Street was passed by.

Bolton was described in the press as being moderately darkened, with the visitor appearing at 12.15 a.m.

When the war came to the North Midlands town of Bolton on 25th & 26th September 1916 ... About 12.20 the sound of explosions was heard ... many people thought it was thunder ... but this was soon dispelled by the sound of 'throbbing' engines.

A police inspector reported that he heard the first explosion at about 12.30 a.m., two-and-a-half minutes later he heard the engines, and it was 8–10 minutes from the first explosion until the last.

'We dressed hurriedly and more or less crowded in the street in real excitement ... wondering what the cause was'... A succession of small explosions led up to a small fusillade followed by others at intervals ... gradually the rhythmic throb of the engines grew fainter.

At Astley Bridge, 17-year-old May Brendal lived with her mother, who ran the sweet shop near to the now demolished 'The Belle' cinema on Belmont Road

Hearing a strange noise outside, looked out and on seeing the *Zepp*, finding the experience terrifying called inside, 'Mother come and look at this', who went to the window and replied with remarkable foresight, 'Get up and look, see this is history'. Outside there were lots of people outside watching L21 appearing quite low and huge whirring overhead.

May had also discerned what she likened to little wheels on the Zeppelin, these were most likely to be the propellers out on the sides. The following morning walking to her job at Eagley Spinning mill, the Zeppelin, having awoken the whole town, was apparently the only subject of conversation.

Another eyewitness from Belmont Road was a 16-year-old baker who was awakened by a policeman knocking on his door 'Come on the Zeppelins are here ... Put your fire out'. He went out in what he describes as brilliant moon light, walking with the constable a short way to the middle of the road to watch as he describes the 'huge silver Cigar, drifting towards the town ... seeing the flames around Trinity Church'. Though, he does go on to state that he believed the bombs to be large iron baskets filled with waste and petrol, which were lit and dropped.

Shortly after passing over here, an incendiary exploded in a field near Sharples Park and Eden Orphanage on Thorns Road. The children were evacuated until the fire was out and Zeppelin gone.

Approximately seven recorded bombs were dropped between Astley Bridge and Queens Park. Passing over Halliwell, the location of many large cotton mills. these bombs caused no deaths but injured three people with shock and bruises, caused structural damage and broke a large number of windows. Sleepers not roused by the first explosions were soon aware of the throbbing sound of the engines as Frankenberg headed southward.

The then four-year-old Marjorie Crompton later remembered being carried out into the garden wrapped in a blanket to the 'Seppelins going across the skyline like big silver cigars … they didn't make any noise they sailed across the sky, it was a very eerie experience'.

As L21 moved over the town, curiosity drew thousands of people to their windows and onto the streets to observe the monster of the sky.

Hobart Street, off Halliwell Road: Terraced Houses near Falcon Mill – 1 explosive bomb.

Darley Street: 1 incendiary bomb near to Richard Harwood & Sons fine cotton spinning mill at Brownlow fold.

Lodge Vale: The end terraced cottage was struck with three ladies resident inside. One widow was caught up in the wreckage of the cottage, being trapped beneath a large beam that rested on a partly collapsed section of wall for half an hour until she could be extracted by rescuers and received medical attention for shock – 1 explosive bomb.

Mortfield Bleach Works Lodges: 1 explosive bomb.

Waldeck Street, off Chorley old Road: 1 incendiary bomb – just north of Halliwell Cotton Works.

Chorley Old Road: An incendiary hit Chorley Old Road opposite Avenue Street. Here it was reported that a mill worker had caused his colleagues great concern by his bold actions in leaving the mill with a bucket of water, dousing the incendiary burning away on a tram track, 20 yards from Halliwell Cotton Works. The man then waited until it had cooled, then, equally coolly, took it away as a souvenir.

Queens Park: An explosive bomb fell into flowerbeds in but failed to explode.

Hobart Street with Eagley Mill at Astley Bridge in the background.

Lodge Vale. (© Bolton Council. From the Collection of Bolton Library and Museum Services)

Piece of tarred rope, a contorted internal metal from the benzol section of a Goldschmidt incendiary. In Bolton Museum's Collection. (© Scott Carter-Clavell)

Another account is related interestingly through the eyes of a then six-year-old who watched the raider from her home at Kensington Place at the junction of St Georges Road and Marsden Road, north-east of the infirmary and Queens Park.

> I looked out the window and there coming along was a great huge balloon ... I said 'ooh look a beautiful big balloon for my Birthday!' Anyhow, and then all the lights came on it ... It dropped some bombs... I thought were fireworks for my birthday ... I heard a lot of people outside shouting. 'Oh dear' you know ... I was told the following morning, that ... they were sorry to tell me it hadn't been a birthday balloon ...
>
> Heading southward L21 started to circle, turning round in a big arc this was witnessed by many below many accounts differ as to the number of circuits, I would put it as one.

It was at this point the Derby Street School log records that L21 made a circuit over the park, seeing that it was undefended and with a free reign above, most likely, attempted to identify serious targets, there is no definitive sequential chronology of the attack, so I have listed the bombed areas in the most plausible sense by plotting the potential route taking into account the loop over the town mentioned by witnesses.

Bolton from Queens Park on a pre-war postcard. In the centre is the fire station on Marsden Road with Town Hall behind. On the right centre ground is the Corn Mill on Spa Road.

Wellington Yard and Street: 2 houses damaged by 2 incendiaries.

From Queens Park Frankenberg had passed over the railway lines, the River Croal, the gasworks and holders on the northern side of the Bullfield Railway sidings.

Next the large structure of Wellington Yard. One incendiary bomb fell into the yard area causing no damage, but in Wellington Street a house received another incendiary through the roof and upper floor, setting alight to the ground floor rooms. Fortunately for the woman and her two children upstairs, they were uninjured as the Fire Brigade were not very far away and doused the flames allowing their escape.

An incendiary bomb that evidently had only partly lit or failed to ignite was found by two young men in their backyard, who put it in a bucket of water and carried the bucket between them on a broom handle to the town hall.

In Wellington Street, a bomb passed through a residence containing 15 people, wrecking the interior. Luckily the bomb did not detonate, and the occupants escaped with their lives and rushed outside – one of them remarking that the Zeppelin looked like a mighty pigeon, and if someone had a gun they could have struck it. Here it was stated that the airship directed light onto the houses for a short time before dropping bombs onto the streets where the deaths happened.

L21 was heading for an area of packed terraced houses and industry including Atlas forge, Soho Iron Works and another large railway junction in addition to at least six large mills in the immediate area.

John St Area: George Owen, then living in Harris Street, later remembered the Zeppelin coming over and an incendiary hitting a stable in 'Penningtons Yard' in the vicinity of the John Street area where horses for the army were apparently being kept. The stable hit by the incendiary was housing a sick horse when it was hit, killing the horse inside. There is no record that the bomb ignited.

Kirk Street: This area was filled with identical brick-built terraced houses of four rooms each (two up, two down).

Kirk Street was located on the western side of the University of Bolton's Deane Campus near to College Way. The 1960s' square buildings on the eastern side sit

Bolton 1920s Bessemers would have been centre bottom, Wellington Street is top centre left. (© Bolton Council. From the collection of Bolton Library and Museum Services)

The gasholders survived another 100 years until their demolition in early 2016. (© Scott Carter-Clavell)

(© Bolton Council. From the Collection of Bolton Library and Museum Services)

on the site of Kirk Street, with no evidence left save for some shops facing the top of College Way that still have the arched doorways seen in the photographs.

Located off Deane Road at the southern end, this was in the general proximity of three large mills, Deane Road Mill, Eagle Mill and Mather Street Mill. It is probable that these were the target, if not the large railway sidings on the eastern side of Mather Street Mill.

Five explosives fell in Kirk Street and five houses were completely destroyed, incorporating Nos 58 to 66.

A total of 13 people were killed, 9 were critically wounded; 19 families were rendered homeless. The noise and concussions roused the entire neighbourhood, rattling the glasses of the Roundcroft Tavern in James Street.

The *Chronicle* reported that end to end the street bore the multitudinous marks from where flying debris had impinged itselves in walls and doors. Many had been wrenched off and window frames forced from buildings. There was not an unbroken pane of glass in Kirk Street or surrounding thoroughfares.

Several houses looked like they'd been struck with a giant's hammer, changed from all semblance of their former shape and condition, as the homes of hard-working artisan people. One witness reported that there was a burst as if the heavens were coming down, and we prepared ourselves for death.

There are many graphic descriptions of the destruction and death that occurred in Kirk Street; reported by the *Bolton Evening News* that night. This had to pass the censor, which it did and, in 1918, it was elaborated upon.

Four bombs, all explosive ... had confined their actual violence to six or eight homes, the terrific impact and vibration had a remarkable impact on two whole streets, probably some two hundred cottages in all. Doors had been wrenched clean off their hinges and hurled into rooms beyond. All windows were shattered and even the frames splintered ... in an upstairs room of one house a bulky chest of drawers had been hurled across the but an elderly lady who usually occupied the room had only recently transferred to sleeping downstairs because of her rheumatism and to this chance it is possible that she owed her life ... An ex-soldier in one of the stricken houses was sitting in a chair when he was flung from one side of the room to the other. On coming to his senses he attempted to release a woman and her baby trapped in another room by debris, but by the time they were extracted they were dead ... but firemen did manage to rescue another two little children trapped but protected by rafters which held off the debris that otherwise would have crushed them.

A newspaper report on the following day emotively delivered a report of the damage, clearly attempting to translate the destruction through the written word but without conveying the actual human loss that occurred. Outlining in great detail the plight of this 'workers' colony', describing the houses as cottages rather than terraces; the revelation that unbroken windows in the street are not to be found leads to a culminating statement in magnificent Edwardian language to describe the southern end of the street.

> What was yesterday the centre of a worker's colony, rows and rows of cottages is today a scene of woebegone desolation. One walks the whole length of the street without seeing an unbroken window and at the southern end is a vista of wanton havoc.

Six four-roomed cottages had become a heap of ruins and for hours firemen, constables (both special and regular), St Johns' ambulance men and members of the women's relief corps assisted by a few soldiers and civilians, worked without ceasing among the debris, searching for crushed and mangled bodies of the victims of blind Hun hate.

John Street – Back James Street: The surrounding streets were blasted by the concussions and very few windows were left unbroken and many splinters had shattered many windows.

Back Apple Street: 1 explosive bomb damaged houses and destroyed outhouses in Back Apple Street.

Looking south at the turn in Kirk Street towards Derby Street. (© Bolton Council. From the collection of Bolton Library and Museum Services)

Kirk Street looking north to Deane Road. (© Bolton Council. From the collection of Bolton Library and Museum Services)

Kirk Street looking north to Deane Road. (© Bolton Council. From the Collection of Bolton Library and Museum Services)

Residents and destruction in Back Apple Street. (© Bolton Council. From the collection of Bolton Library and Museum Services)

Damaged outhouses in Back Apple Street. (© Bolton Council. From the collection of Bolton Library and Museum Services)

Moor Mills, Parrot Street adjacent to Apple Street: Over this area, as L21 turned north-east-east, one explosive bomb was aimed at Moor Mills complex, a large cotton mill on the south side adjacent to Parrot Street. This bomb shattered all the windows in the street and on this side of the mill, destroying part of the pavement and catapulting a piece of kerbstone up to and into the fourth storey of the mill.

It was reported after the war that a bomb had dropped near a mill of a thousand looms operated by Messrs Johnson, Hodgkinson and Pearson Ltd – this appears on inquiry to have been at Moor Mills.

An incendiary aimed at Moor Mills hit its mark and penetrated the roof of a storage area, possibly between the two main mill buildings adjacent to an engine house. Messrs Ormrod and Hardcastle suffered fire damage to a large quantity of cotton yarn, though the sprinkler system doused the potential catastrophe. Causing the collapse of a roof and damage to the building neighbouring the engine house. The damage was estimated at £250 (£14,000 in 2016) as only 10 years previously, this mill had suffered a fire, which had cost £2,000–3,000 in repairs. The raid damage evidently caused further trouble for the workers as a former winder of Ormrod and Hardcastle, Mrs Harrison, born in 1900 and interviewed in the 1980s, described that some workers had suffered lacerated feet from the broken windows over the floor. As many spinners and piecers went barefoot due to the oil on the floor and could easily pick up bits of stray cotton between toes instead of bending down to pick them up. In her words, this 'handicapped them for life'.

Cotton Mill Winding Room.

As a consequence, many left, and she was rapidly elevated to a position where she was looking after winding and clearing frames trimming the yarn – stopping overflows, which if had been left unattended could have been hundreds of miles of yarn, had she not been attentive to the automatically flowing frames throughout two winding rooms. This occupied her throughout the rest of the war.

It was recorded in the *Chronicle* a few days later that the craft changed altitude frequently and at times it was clearly discerned, in addition to the explosive and incendiary bombs, star shells were sent down – it would seem possible, albeit foolish, to send down a parachute flare if at this point they believed they were over the eastern counties, where the home defence airfields were situated.

Back Deane Road between Fern Street and Washington Street: An L21 circling over the town was said by one witness to be 1,000 yards in length. Passing over the vicarage, where the Revd Henry John Jauncey and his wife Charlotte resided for St Saviour's Church near Deane Road, who were still in mourning for the loss of their son Sub Lt Henry Jauncey killed at Jutland. The church was demolished in 1975. The huge complexes of cotton mills such as Swan Lane here were missed or passed by in favour of going for the forges again.

Moor Mills at Parrot Street. (© Bolton Council. From the collection of Bolton Library and Museum Services)

Spinners & Piecers repairing yarn on a 1286 Spindle Fine Cotton Spinning Mule, similar to those at Moor Mills.

L21 would have been turning south near or over Rosamund Street, off St Helens Road, where a 10-year-old girl was living with her grandparents. A weaver in later life, she recalled the events she had witnessed. Her grandfather was a miner who worked nights, so she slept in with bed-ridden grandmother alongside a constant light that kept burning for her. They were awakened by shouts outside of 'turn you lights out – turn you lights out' not knowing why the girl duly did so, as they heard a bang, only for it to shortly become clear what was happening.

The next bomb dropped behind Deane Road, severely damaging the Co-operative laundry building breaking the windows, roof and boiler house, which caused several problems in later years for the owners according to the correspondence of Bradshaw, Gass and Hope. Also it was said to have killed all the ducks in the Laundry yard.

Holy Trinity Church: The next target may have been the Soho Iron Works or the Yorkshire and Lancashire Railway immediately behind, but these were not hit, the large bomb instead plummeted through the roof of Holy Trinity Church, which was situated between the two. This did not explode but simply burst open after badly damaging an upper-level gallery and destroying several pews.

The diary of the verger Thomas Sanderson records his discovery:

Zeppelins visit to Bolton; 8:30 a.m. Tuesday;
Describing on Entering the church, and seeing damage and disorder within. The interior of the church had been covered in a film of yellow dust – Walking down

the Nave he kicked a bit of the shell casing – the bomb had not exploded but had burst open through the south east corner bursting open in the process but destroying a number of pews under the gallery.

Half of the bomb was discovered under a pew underneath the gallery still containing Mr Sanderson approximated three pounds of TNT. Informing the Vicar very quickly and the Police just after 9 a.m. the clean-up was evidently a slow process no doubt due to the explosive powder everywhere as over the next few days more parts of the bomb were discovered and taken to the Police Station.

The powder is certainly from a Carbonite bomb. An explosive compound composed of Nitro-glycerine, Nitrobenzene, Saltpetre and Sulphur which most likely accounted for the yellow appearance of the powder, traces may be seen on thread of the nose cone below.

Bomb fragments from Holy Trinity church held in Bolton Museum Collection. (Images © Scott Carter-Clavell)

Postcard of Holy Trinity church from around 1910.

Nose cone of a dud 110IB Carbonit bomb. (© Scott Carter-Clavell)

(© Bolton Council. From the
collection of Bolton Library
and Museum Services)

Town Centre

Heading north across Crook Street, the final area subjected to attack was the
streets in the vicinity of the Town Hall. The Town Hall being a tall and substantial
structure would have been visible enough to warrant a bomb or two. Bessemers
lay just behind the Town Hall on Moor Lane and was missed completely.

They did not hit the great structure but the first incendiary hit Johnson's
wholesale fruit warehouse, situated at the junction of Ashburner and Old Hall
Street South about 50 yards from the south side of the Town Hall.

A second went through the roof of Messrs Haughton solicitor's office in
Mawdsley Street, which was quelled before any real damage occurred. The last
explosive, said to be a dud, fell on Mealhouse Lane. This was the last German
bomb to fall on Bolton until 1941. Although, strangely, this last one is not marked
upon the official 1916 map of the bombs on Bolton.

The airship turned northward andwas probably heading away from the Town
Hall, when they would have passed near James Chadwick's Ironfounders at School
Hill. At this time, Chadwick's were producing the infamous 'toffee apple' trench
mortar bomb by the thousand. The bombing run over Bolton only lasted in the
region of 10 minutes, according to a policeman.

The thousands of eyes drawn to windows, sliding up the sash windows peering
out in the darkness, running outside to see what the 'ell is that. Fears overridden
by curiosity and concern. Word spread quickly as to what had happened, rumours
spreading via the 'grimy night toilers' returning to their homes all over passing
word to the many outdoors and the inquisitive enquirers.

Destruction, houses collapsed crowds and, as what must have been thousands
of people in night clothes, hurriedly dressed, all wearing clogs, headed out into
chilled night air down the darkened alleys, thoroughfares and roads. This made

Aerial shot of the Town Hall area around 1927. Note the buildings darkened by soot. The large space behind the Town Hall is where Bessemers was situated.

Bolton Town Hall, 1902. (© Bolton Council. From the collection of Bolton Library and Museum Services)

Right: The Wholesale Warehouse and Town Hall in 1910. (© Bolton Council. From the collection of Bolton Library and Museum Services)

Below: Area of the last bomb of the raid. (© Bolton Council. From the collection of Bolton Library and Museum Services)

a real clattering din as the many thousand clog irons clattered on the pavements, cobbles and roads from the surrounding streets and areas.

Some gathered at points where explosives or incendiaries had landed in the streets but the majority headed for the Kirk Street area. Throughout the rest of the night, it was almost impossible to get near the affected streets. The noise of this alone would have drowned out the engines of an approaching airship, fortunately L21 had no intention of returning. Those in the crowds of a more nervous or excitable nature were said to have dived for cover on the odd rumour the *Zepp* was coming back. Most of the onlookers were said to have stayed until morning in the vicinity held by the cordons, swapping stories and experiences.

Many pieces of shrapnel had been picked up along with some dud incendiaries and handed in to the police and council officials, the army disposed of the unexploded bombs, though some bits were kept as souvenirs.

A wooden box which contains the piece of incendiary at Bolton Museum. (Image © Scott Carter-Clavell)

Return to Nordholz

It is stated in the official report that L21 was visible from Atherton at 12.40 a.m. – if this is accurate then this could be at the final point of the attack just before she went northwards.

L21's homeward route was seemingly unremarkable, making a course past Blackburn, where it was reported at 1.00 a.m.

It was reported after the war in the *Burnley Express* that some residents of Burnley were awakened by the noise of the Zeppelin engines directly above the town, with some claiming they had seen a dim grey shape above.

The last-known explosive bomb was dropped at Bolton Abbey, which did not detonate at 1.35 a.m. L21 made a more-or-less straight north-easterly course skirting Ripon at 2 a.m. and Thirsk at 2.15 a.m., over the North Yorkshire Moors and was seen heading out to sea near Whitby at 3.05 a.m.

The following week the *Whitby Gazette* quietly reported that a man living on the east coast had been fined 40s for leaving an electric light on and door open, as he rushed out to see a Zeppelin overhead returning to Germany on the previous weekend.

By any means this was a redoubtable feat, once returned to Nordholz, L21 had completed a flight of nearly 1,000 miles.

Due caution of Peter Strasser after the previous night's losses, the Zeppelins orders had meant they had avoided the areas with the heaviest concentrations

L21 in January 1916 at Nordholz Note the man walking along the top of L21. (© Nordholz Aeronauticum)

of home defence aircraft. Defensive patrols by RFC and RNAS aircraft had been futile, with only L31 being spotted near Portsmouth by two flying boats unable to pursue.

Heavier Losses: Bolton did not suffer the heaviest loss of life that night, Sheffield suffered its first raid by L22 commanded by Martin Dietrich, which dropped 36 bombs killing 28 people including 7 members of 1 family, seriously damaging 89 houses with a 150 others incurring slight damage. Dietrich had been unsure as to whether he was over Lincoln or Sheffield. As in Bolton, though a large industrial centre, all the bombs fell on residential properties.

CHAPTER 7

'A VISTA OF WANTON HAVOC': ACCOUNTS AND REPORTS FROM BOLTON

Kirk Street Victims and Witnesses

Rescue work had begun shortly after the initial bombardment; owing to the fragile nature of the damaged buildings, the search teams worked in relays until 1.30 p.m. on Wednesday, once everyone was accounted for, after a lodger from one of the ruined residences had been away in another town, and it wasn't clear to the search teams that this was the case.

The rescuers from different services, special constables, firemen and neighbours started searching, as they could hear moans from the rubble. They quickly brought two children out alive, but their task was to become a solemn one of trying to bring out and help the injured, the dying and the shocked. The 13 dead were subsequently listed as the following:

Men: An ironworker aged 43,
An ironworker aged 42,
A warehouseman aged 34,
A packing-case maker aged 62 (died in the infirmary),
A labourer (who was a lodger) aged 36,
Women: A mother of five children aged 44,
A baby (daughter of the above) aged 2 ½,
A married woman aged 40,
A daughter of the above aged 5,
A married woman aged 32,
A mother of three children aged 42,
A weaver (daughter of the above) aged 17

No. 58 Kirk Street: Bridget, 44, and Margaret Irwin, 2½ – The terraced house occupied by Joseph and Bridget Irwin and their family was hit by the explosive. Having retired to bed at 9.30 p.m., their sleep was shattered by the upper walls, and ceiling collapsing onto the bed and the floor giving way. The bed and three occupants fell through into the living room beneath. When a neighbour reached them, Joseph had managed to extract himself, but Bridget was pinned underneath the bed holding her baby tightly – the neighbour recounted that if there had been immediate help, she could have been got out alive, but in the way of the structural collapse of the building, more debris fell on top of the stuck pair, denying the chance to extricate them, and it was a while before a concerted effort recovered them. By this time unfortunately, Bridget was dead and Margaret died shortly afterwards.

In this house, there were four other children: two boys and two girls – Annie, Joe, Jack and Letitia – who climbed out on to the roof of an adjoining building to climb down and run, shivering with fright into the house across the road. The lady who greeted the children into the safety of her home had been awakened by the explosions and shattering of all of her windows. The lady went on to state that her wall clock had stopped bang on 12.40, though it had been 10 minutes fast.

A sister of Bridget lived in the street nearby with her eight children. She searched the rubble in the daylight for the possessions and photographs of her sister's family to save. Recounting her experience to a journalist, her tale of being nearly thrown out of bed by the concussion, her husband apparently was pessimistic of their chances saying, 'let's stop where we are, we are done for' before running to the back room, as another explosion close by the houses went off, in doing so wrenching the room door off its hinges into her husband's face almost knocking him over. The lady said, 'I'm thankful the baby-slayers did not hurt my little ones'.

No. 60 Kirk Street: Husband and wife Michael, 42, an iron worker, and Martha O'Hara, 41, a shop keeper, were killed next door.

At one of the houses where two parents were killed, it was reported that four children huddled under a table in the kitchen to save themselves from the debris as the house collapsed.

No. 62 Kirk Street: William, 42, an ironworker, and Ann McDermott, 36, and their five-year-old daughter, Mary Ellen (Nellie) were killed.

No. 64 Kirk Street: Mr and Mrs James Allison and their lodgers, Frederick James Guildford, 62, and David Davis, 39, were killed too. Frederick died later at the Bolton Royal Infirmary. He was a packing-case maker and David was a coal heaver.

No. 66 Kirk Street: The Gregory family was inside when the house was virtually eviscerated. The family inside was instantly shattered as the 17-year-old daughter, a weaver, was killed outright; her mother Elizabeth, 42, was rescued alive but died of shock after being taken into a neighbouring house. The father a railwayman was evacuated with cuts to the head, but it wasn't until seven o' clock that the 18-month old son was retrieved without suffering severe physical injury. During his ordeal, the rescuers had been able to speak to the boy and pass food to him.

Other accounts were published anonymously in the press.

A family living next door to a destroyed property escaped total annihilation and were extricated by rescuers, despite the internal collapse of the walls of the rear bedroom, which contained the mother, father and child huddled in their bed in the darkness for two-and-a-half hours, for fear of further structural failure and the floor collapsing beneath them. They had no light just the sound of the distant voices and hubbub outside. A line of rescuers guided by a fireman carrying an electric torch eventually made their way tentatively up the fragile stairs, 'Thank God someone has come' were the husband's words, on being pulled out of the shambles of splintered wooden beams, plaster, bricks and glass. His wife was unconscious and was carried downstairs by one of the younger of the rescuing party, followed by a fireman who carried the child. They had a very lucky escape.

Ex-Constable
The house of an ex-policeman of the Bolton force 'was converted to fantastic Topsyturveydom' with effects of two explosions at the back of the property, flinging the man across a room violently into a wall. In among the detritus of his home, amid smashed crockery and a glass cabinet, he was unscathed apart from shock and effects of inhaling the foul gases given off by the bomb, and managed to get a look at the assailant as it went over which he described as 'a great lumbering thing which he could have almost shot with a rifle'.

Mother and Son
Close to the devastation a mother and her son resided in a terraced house from which they witnessed the bombing:

> I was not a sound sleeper and I was awakened by a tingling sound which caused me to sit up and listen. Then I heard a big report and I called to my son in the back room 'I'm sure there is one over' his reply was 'It's thunder, try and to go to sleep.' Then the crash came and I thought we were done for and I pulled the (bed) clothes over me. I shall never forget it. It's a miracle this house didn't go too. The Window came in and caught my son on the chest and I don't know how he got himself loose. The shock was if the sky was coming down, and prepared ourselves for death. My son heard someone moaning, and he went out and did what he could. Before the crash came there was light that moved about like a snake but my son said it was lightning. As soon as we could we flew through the back and he said 'Mother, it's gone; the danger is over' and I said a prayer of thankfulness that by the mercy of god we had been saved.

A man, an engine-tenter by profession, was caught with his wife at the back of their residence by two explosions that caused the bedroom wall to collapse along with the ceiling. They were said to been trapped unconscious for two hours in the darkness, until coming to, and cries for help led to their discovery.

A greenhouse in the rear yard was obliterated by the blast.

The noise of the Zeppelin engines high above aroused the services in place for such an event.

Police and special constables marshalled the huge crowds drawn to the area to see for themselves the results of the visit. Many people went to the scene working throughout the night with torches searching the rubble; fortunately for the rest of Kirk Street, the gas main had not been ignited and so, fortunately, the fire brigade was not needed in their primary capacity.

Many doctors, ambulance staff, Red Cross nurses and special constables assisted in every way they could to the wounded. A cordon was formed to keep the crowds at bay whose curiosity provided a constant background noise to the rescue efforts. The five seriously injured people were taken to the infirmary as soon as transport arrived including Frederick Guildford, a lodger who later succumbed to his injures.

A journalist commented that it was an experience that will hold a permanent place in the history of the town, as undoubtedly it will be unforgettable by all who witnessed its operations in the clear starlit sky.

There had been various reports of two Zeppelins over the town. Though more likely, the reports were probably from people actually witnessing L21 circumnavigate the town, seeing it disappear and then reappear at a different angle. The nearest other Zeppelins had been L22 over Sheffield and L14 in the Leeds-Wetherby area.

Aerial shot of Bolton Infirmary in the 1920s. (© Bolton Council. From the collection of Bolton Library and Museum Services)

Panorama of Bolton sites.

Elizabeth Andersen – Bolton Women's Relief Corps

A fascinating person worthy of a book herself is Elizabeth Ann Andersen. Born in Darcy Lever, she was a trained teacher working with handicapped children in Manchester as well as being a very active Suffragette, selling *Votes for Women* newspapers in Bolton town centre promoting the Suffragist cause. As in many ways, the war had opened up opportunities for women unthinkable beforehand, Elizabeth on her return from her training in London had become a member of the Manchester Women's Relief Corp and was asked to form a Relief Corp for Bolton by the mayor. Hundreds joined her group, and they learnt many new skills in evenings and weekends such as drill, Morse code, bugle and drumming, first aid and home nursing at their base at Clarence Street Council School.

For the 26-year-old Elizabeth, on the night of the raid she got her chance to put her training to good use. On hearing of the bombing, she raced out to the fire station on Moor Lane, where the Relief Corp kept a first-aid kit, just managing to catch the last fire engine on its way to Kirk Street, and hitched a lift.

> I remember seeing men in nightshirts shinning up lamp posts to put out the gas lights which were still burning and when we reached Kirk Street, where the Zeppelin had dropped bombs, there was a huge mound of rubble from which firemen were rescuing bodies ... To my horror, I found there was no water, the mains had been cut off because of flooding, so I grabbed a teapot and used the drop of tea inside. I then charged round all the cottages, collecting the tea from the pots on the hobs.

Bolton Women's Relief Corps. Elizabeth is seated second from left on the second row (© Bolton Council. From the collection of Bolton Library and Museum Services)

Marsden Road Fire Station, reproduced from an old Frith's Series Postcard, 1903.

None of her fellow ladies appeared at her post, though unbeknown to her the other members had kept the crowds away from the bomb site at Kirk Street with a cordon then assisting the injured in daylight.

Elizabeth worked throughout the night, until being relieved at 6 a.m., after which she caught the train to Manchester to continue her day's teaching.

A diary kept by a doctor at Townley's hospital (now the Royal Bolton Hospital) records in a stereotypical doctor's hand – virtually illegible handwriting:

> This morning I was awoken by a strange sound from the sky ... I called only to hear W running ... 'Look up at a Zeppelin' I ran, more in-joke than anything else...at breakfast all was agog with talk about a Zeppelin raid- *Bolton had been attacked!* ... Deane Road had been bombed and the word was of many deaths, worried about sunny ... was safe or not.

Although working in a local hospital, he makes no mention of any raid casualties, apart from an unrelated convoy of wounded servicemen the next day. He mentions running 'in-joke' to see the Zeppelin in disbelief of what he was hearing. He as many others believed that the Germans could not travel this far north-west and a joke was being played out.

The *Chronicle* published an interview with a man in the Volunteer Training Corps (VTC), who claimed to have had notice of a Zeppelin in the area as early as 11.30 p.m. so as to ready stand pipes and hoses and by 12.10 a.m. when he witnessed explosions. In a 1918 edition of the evening news, it was stated that the Bolton Borough police had received warning of a Zeppelin's presence in the district, the Chief Constable set in motion plans including special constables, ambulance men, Women's Relief Corps, nurses, and some of the munitions works were warned as quickly as telephones would allow. Apparently, the reason that the services were caught off guard was that the previous plans for a raider to get so far inland had not worked. Northern regions had previously relied on southern military command notifying areas of an intruder, but, in this case, as L21 had been essentially wandering blindly over the Peak district and, as the bombing run took about 30–35 minutes at the most to complete, it was a very quick affair with them again disappearing off over the Yorkshire moors and then the coast.

Soldiers, sightseers and artillery near Edgworth Camp near Bolton, 1914.

CHAPTER 8

AFTER THE RAID

GERMAN VERSION.

———

Amsterdam, Tuesday.

The following official communiqué was received here from Berlin:—

On the night of September 25th and 26th, a section of our naval airships lavishly bombarded with explosive and incendiary bombs with visible results the British naval port of Portsmouth, the " reinforced " places at the mouth of the Thames, and the industrial and railway installations of military importance in the centre of England, including York, Leeds, Lincoln, and Derby.

In spite of strong enemy attacks our airships returned undamaged.

(Signed) Chief of Naval Staff.

Newspaper cutting detailing German reports..

The official German press statement that was published nationally is peppered with wild claims and bravado.

The British reports came in throughout the night:

25 September, 11.45 p.m.
Several hostile airships crossed the East and North-East
Coasts between 10.30 and midnight. Bombs are reported to

have been dropped at several places between Northern and
North-Midland Counties. An airship has also been reported
off the South Coast. No reports of damage or casualties have been received.

26 September, 12.10 p.m.
Seven airships carried out a raid on England last night
and in the early hours of this morning. The districts
attacked were the South Coast, East Coast, North-East
Coast and North Midlands. The principal attack was aimed
against the industrial centres in the last-mentioned area.
Up to the present no damage to factories or work of military
importance has been reported. It is reported, however, that
a number of small houses and cottages were wrecked or
damaged in some places, and 29 deaths have been reported.
No attempt was made to approach London. The raiders were engaged by the
anti-aircraft defences and were successfully driven off from several large
industrial centres.

3.15 a.m.
Several hostile airships, probably six in number, visited
the North-Eastern and Southern Counties during the night.
Bombs were dropped in the Northern Counties, and some
casualties and damage are reported. Full reports have not
yet been received.

5.20 p.m.
In the raid of last night-the total casualties so far reported
are: Killed, 36. Injured, 27.
* Very slight damage was caused, and none whatever of
military importance.

The Derby Street School Diary comments that on 26 September, the registers were
not marked on the advice of the supervisor, with 60 children being absent. Fifteen
lived in Kirk Street yet not one was injured!

Most marvellous escapes had been experienced and the calmness and absence
of abnormality on the part of the poor children whose homes had been destroyed
was a wonderful witness to their ability to undergo emergencies.

The school log expands upon the detail, which is quite matter of fact, even
identifying the potential targets that the Zeppelin was most certainly aiming for in
the vicinity such as the gasworks or the town hall, although with no mention of the
railway or the ironworks.

The insignificance of the material damage aside from the loss of life hardly
justified their 'murderous errand'. The report added that £3,000 would be
sufficient cost of repair apart from the loss of life.

Whether the press was censored or not, word-of-mouth could not be restrained, the word spread like wildfire, the curiosity of the much heard about Zeppelin raids drew thousands of people to Bolton rom all over the north and as far as Liverpoolover the following days to see the damaged buildings f. On 27 September, the streets were filled with sightseers from morning until dusk, with every type of road-going transport in their efforts:

> Numbers of families were housed and fed in the Flash Street special school and the benevolence of the town was showered upon the unfortunate sufferers in no stinted manner.

A mule spinner later described visiting Kirk Street afterwards and seeing sheets being put out for people to throw pennies into for the injured and homeless as he toured the bomb sites on his bicycle. Many people collected the various parts of burst duds or shrapnel from the hit areas and kept them as souvenirs or handed them in at the police station or town hall.

> Some of the sightseers being former residents will no doubt have been glad to have not be still living in Bolton such as Frederick Livingstone a Mule Spinner who had been born in Lodge vale in 1874 and later his daughter Alice had been born in Waldeck St in 1909 before moving to Leigh.

The young birthday balloon witness at Kensington Place recalled visiting the site:

> It was German Zeppelin … had bombed Kirk Street off Deane road … the following Sunday we all went and mum gave us a penny each and she said … 'I'm going to make you go and see all this devastation' and there was a big canvas box arrangement and we all had to throw our money in to help them.

Carbonit bomb fragment at Bolton Museum. (Image © Scott Carter-Clavell)

She was reassured by her family that the 'Naughty balloon' had been brought down by a battery of guns over the moors and was gone!

The official GHQ Intelligence section compiled reports on every raid and the plotted routes of every Zeppelin. It was noted that in Bolton 'One Fire, not serious was caused at a Mill …'. No damage was done to the Bessemer Steel Forge or any factories or public buildings.

Frankenberg's Report

Frankenberg's report written on 26 September at Nordholz is rather short; however, this may be due to the apparent trouble in navigating, as he mentions trouble in getting a fix on their position; however, he was assisted in approaching the coast by the lighthouses at Cromer and Harborough [sic] possibly Happisburgh on the Norfolk coast making land at 'Chapel' (-Street Leonards).

He reported that he attacked blast furnaces at Derby with 2,000 kg explosives and the success was good to watch. Reporting that the town was undefended but had received fire over Nottingham and near the coast – possibly attributable to the flashes of mill boilers lighting up in the distance appearing as flashes of gunfire. He states later that it was impossible to orientate themselves, though after receiving a direction, finding they were considerably off course. This shows clearly that there were some navigational problems on board. Most likely from when they reached Sheffield and avoiding the city, as Frankenberg seems to have been quite a careful commander in his previous raids, sticking to the east coast areas around Norfolk, Suffolk and Lincolnshire, as it was a daring change of tactic to head for the north west. Stating Derby as the target may indicate that they thought they were still over the eastern counties.

The speed at which the raid happened doesn't appear to be unusual, as in Mathy's interview a year earlier he mentions this:

> *KvW:* 'How long were you over London?' I asked the lieutenant commander …
> *Hm:*   'The main attack was from 10.50 to 11, just ten minutes.'
> *KvW:* 'Then the Zeppelin tactics of attack are to make a dash to points to be bombarded and quickly get away?'
> *Hm:*   'Yes, attacks must be short and quick."

That night on board L21 there may be a relatively simple reason why the Zeppelin ended up over Bolton as no gyro-compasses were carried on airships due to weight restrictions; however, liquid-magnetic-type compasses made by Carl Bamburg of Berlin were fitted. These were situated near the *Steurman* in the control gondola on gimbals, which gave stability. In the low temperatures, these primitive liquid compasses tended to freeze in the higher altitudes, despite the addition of alcohol. There was a small lamp situated within the base body of the compass to illuminate the radium arrows on the face that indicated directions. It was said that the lamps

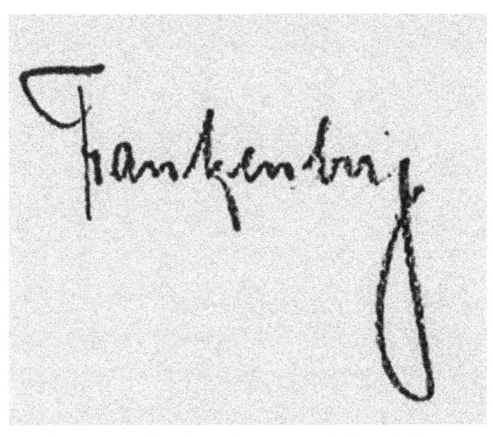

Frankenberg's signature on the raid report. (© Aeronauticum Luftschiffe Nordholz)

L21 over Nordholz. (© Aeronauticum Luftschiffe Nordholz)

were sometimes used to try and thaw the frozen compasses; however, in an all-metal structure in sub-zero temperatures it is doubtful it would have much effect. So a frozen compass and bad reception for radio waves meant they approximated their position in in the wrong direction.

The bombing pattern over Holcombe and Kirk Street Bolton was rapid, this may have been due to problems with the electric bomb release gear, as testified to by the captured 'electrical fitter' from L33, who claimed that the release mechanisms needed constant attention. Therefore, some bombs may have been dropped by hand.

The irony of this is that Frankenberg had inadvertently bombed Derby earlier in his operational career on 1 February 1916, while as executive officer on the L14 yet after that raid in his report Cdr Bocker claimed Liverpool had been hit. In April 1918, when Wigan was bombed by L61, Cdr Ehrlich reported he had bombed Sheffield.

Oberleutnant Zur See
Kurt Frankenberg.
(© Aeronauticum Luftschiffe
Nordholz)

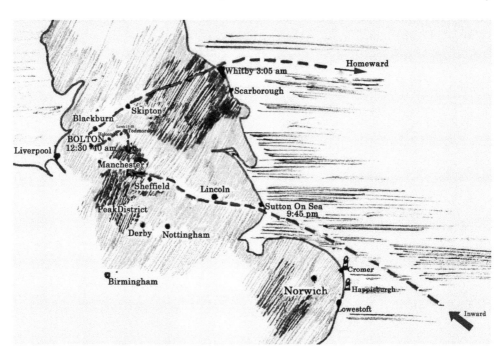

© Scott Carter-Cavell

Inquest and Verdict as Reported in the Press

Pieces of bombs were collected and assembled on a table at the coroner's inquest on the following Thursday, after the raid. They had been catalogued with labels attached describing where they had been found and the finder's name. Some pieces were said to be a quarter of an inch thick.

There were expressions of sympathy from the coroner with families of the deceased and he voiced his hope for justice and punishment. The Jury then viewed the bodies at the Hospital mortuary, which must have been a very demanding ordeal for those loved ones present, as some of the victims bore the scares plainly and in some cases facially and others were said to look like they were asleep only 'the pallor of death' showed it was not so. The identification of the bodies was done by relatives, in-laws and acquaintances.

Medical evidence to the coroner was supplied in the form of the infirmary's surgeons declaration that one young girl's cause of death was asphyxiation due to burial in the debris of her home. A male's death was said to be caused not only in part by shock but also by brain damage due to being buried in the wreckage.

A witness provided evidence regarding the lighting and echoes what Elizabeth Andersen witnessed on sighting lights going out; he climbed up and extinguished three street lamps and at Kirk Street seeing 30 men getting people out assisted by the witness. The coroner specifically asked if the lighting adhered to the regulations with the exception of flare from an unnamed place, probably Bessemer's works, there was nothing beyond the usual light to which the answer was 'No'.

A police inspector testified as to seeing there being only one airship at 800–1,000 yards up not displaying any lights. In time from the first bomb to the last exploding it was about 8–10 minutes long.

The question of defences had been raised and dropped, it was not thought wise as there were too many spies in England for information regarding defences to be discussed, so it would not end up being transmitted abroad and benefiting the enemy.

A question was asked by a jury member was: 'Is there a system to give warning of the approach of the Zeppelins' to which the answer was in the positive from the coroner adding that 'Unfortunately many people believed that Zeppelins couldn't actually travel very far', continuing to suggest that these events would spur them on to greater precautions, yet the authorities are sufficiently awaee of all the circumstances. Amid more expressions of sympathy, reports were given as to the turning out of the rescuers and Fire Brigade. This was followed by the Mayor James Seddon adding his sympathies towards the families of the dead, and he voiced his hope that more citizens would assist in helping him assist those suffering from the raid. The jury returned a verdict of death as a result of injuries through missiles dropped from an aircraft.

The mayor's comments were supported by his writing to local newspapers appealing for a liberal response to the urgent need of the homeless and shattered families for clothing and wearing apparel of every description, as well as bedding and furniture. He wrote that it should be delivered to the Town Hall or he will arrange collection. Not far from this appeal in one newspaper was a report of a communique announcing that London to be destroyed from the air.

Funerals

On the following Saturday, thousands of people gathered for the services and internments of the victims of the bombings at Tongue and Heaton Cemeteries.

At Heaton, for the internments of Ellen and Elizabeth Gregory and Frederick James Guildford that took place, the roads were lined with people from Kirk Street to the gates of the cemetery.

One of the ironworkers (Wm McDermott or Michael O'Hara) had his funeral paid for by work colleagues contributing from their wages, which raised £42 (about £2,000 today) and they paid for the flowers of his and of the other ironworker. Sixty ironworkers followed the coffin in solemn lines behind the cortege to Tongue Cemetery.

The mayor, who was present at all the burials, said at this man's grave having seen the procession of workers: 'Here was one beloved of many and what a lesson to everyone when fathers, mothers and children have been killed without any warning at all. We must try and live well and to do good, we must live as brothers in fellowship with God as with man and must be prepared for whatever might come.'

For the others being laid to rest many followed the procession, with 200 members of the Women of the Blessed Sacrament paying their respects following the cortege. A non-conformist was also interred at Tongue mourned by many of his fellow workers.

The Catholic priest conducting these services was reported as saying:

We have seen how 'brave' German soldiers fought, here was witnessed how the culture and education of Germany had writ itself large upon our life to-day. The 'brave' soldiers had struck at the child, at the mother at the defenceless man, at everything we had been taught through the English Canons of Sentiment had taught the English to revere ...

We had been taught how to defend the weak and the defenceless and to stay the hand of him who would strike. The Germans were the people asking us to model our education system upon their system. Save Us from Germany.

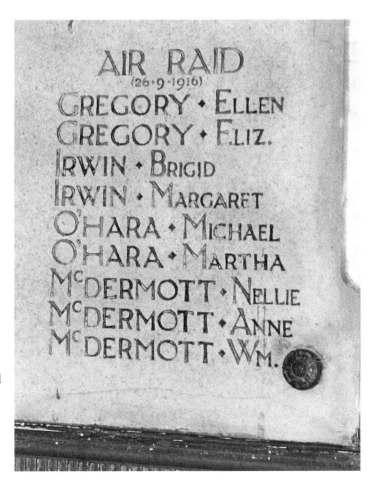

The 1914–18 memorial in St Peter and St Pauls Roman Catholic Church in Pilkington Street not far from Kirk Street. (Photo © Julie Lamara)

CHAPTER 9

AFTERWARDS

Town Defence

Immediately following the raid, the Chief Constable Fred Mullineux had notices put in the papers instructing members of various groups on the alarm being given of 'Hostile Aircraft' and detailing where to assemble in case of air raid. For members of the Special Constable company's No. 1 at Mr Kay's office; No. 2 at Town Hall; No. 3 Dobson and Barlows works. No. 4 at Silverwell Street Drill hall and No. 5 at the tram shed on Bradshawgate; VTC at the drill hall in Silverwell Street; Women's Relief Corp at the Fire Station on Marsden Road and a section of Red Cross nurses at the Town Hall.

Though things returned to normal, for the majority, there was an awareness that they too were vulnerable like other places they'd read about, chatted about sons, cried about friends, boyfriends, lovers, fiancés, brothers, fathers, cousins away somewhere unknown, all with the knowledge some wouldn't be returning, and just hope that the rest would safely come back. It had been a bloody year. On 2 October, the town clerk wrote to the war office after a meeting of the town watch committee in regards to providing some means of AA protection for the town. Receiving no reply, he sent another letter on 24 November; eventually, receiving a reply from Maj.-Gen. Shaw of the General Staff at the GHQ of Home Forces in Whitehall, dated 1 December, stating that the Field Marshal C in C Sir John French would like to state that 'the protection of the country is not being overlooked but it is impossible to afford protection for every individual town'.

By this point in the war, early in December, Zeppelin activity was heavily reduced after an extremely bloody year. To date there had been 42 airship raids; yet, with the airship threat apparently controlled, plans were afoot in the higher British echelons to halt the supply of AA guns to towns, while equipping merchant shipping against the inherently more dangerous U-boats, and redirect home defence squadrons to the Western Front.

Further up the valley in Ramsbottom, where L21 had passed over, lighting restrictions were imposed and street kerbs painted white. Whereas, in Haslingden, Alderman Worsley, chairman of the Lighting Committee proposed not to light any street lamps during the coming winter time and lamps post were to be painted white to a height of 4 feet.

In neighbouring Bury, the town council meeting in October was warned of the dangers of dark nights, as reports emerged that people had been walking into unlit lampposts and banging their faces. These were ordered to be painted white along with kerbstones, though some had gone further and painted the gable ends of houses white.

In the weeks following the raid, amid the notices for those killed in action and missing, the Bolton papers printed instructions on warnings if the town was raided again. The signal for a raid was the same as in other regions, the alert would go out by the gasworks lowering the gas supply pressure in three waves, with three seconds between each wave then the pressure would be left at half. A very similar arrangement with the electricity would take place but with the supply being turned off completely. After these signals people were instructed to extinguish all gas lights.

This did not go uncriticised:

Frank Smith of 278 Wigan Road wrote on behalf of concerned Boltonians in complaining to the readers of the *Chronicle* of the decision to leave the gas at half pressure after an alert, thus leaving street lamps illuminated giving the enemy a 'sure guide' arguing that complete darkness is the best defence, so not as to be found in 'a hopeless muddle as in one 'North Midlands Town' (Bolton) recently. Finishing the statement, he implores 'this is no time for half measures, we must take every precaution to thwart the inhuman devices of our despicable foe'.

Another concerned resident wrote to the paper complaining about the necessity for absolute darkness in the town at night, as the disgraceful allowance of glares and flashes from many mills' boiler houses should be stopped and legislated against by the authorities.

An anonymous, yet pointed, suggestion appeared in local papers of the affected districts, a few days after purporting to be from a resident concerned at the prospect of further raids.

The section suggests that the authorities and population work together. Preparedness gives confidence and so other northern towns are not caught napping not falling to the arch murderer's desires – nervousness and terror. The main suggestions centre on the use of designated cellars as refuges and other safe areas in the event of a raid. Evidently, the author sought to allay that very morbid Victorian fear of being buried alive, as he/she suggests if cellars are used then there should be a system of mutual checks by neighbouring parties to determine the condition of the cellars and occupants. In reference to the authorities who should be giving ample warning of a raid ending with that it should be decided on without further delay.

An advantage to both sides that was used throughout the Zeppelin raids was propaganda. After the raid on Bolton, a local printer produced such cards with a description.

Whereas in Germany propaganda would have taken place in a similar vein, though going further than in Britain, such as publishing photographs of dead

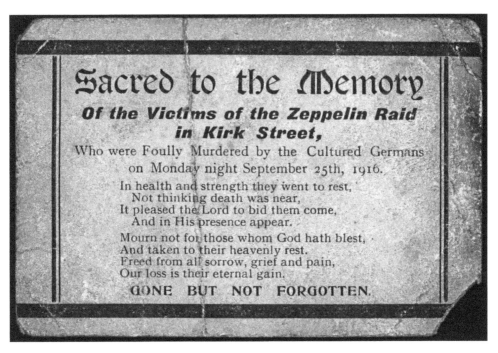

Sacred to the Memory
Of the Victims of the Zeppelin Raid
in Kirk Street,
Who were Foully Murdered by the Cultured Germans
on Monday night September 25th, 1916.
In health and strength they went to rest,
Not thinking death was near,
It pleased the Lord to bid them come,
And in His presence appear.
Mourn not for those whom God hath blest,
And taken to their heavenly rest.
Freed from all sorrow, grief and pain,
Our loss is their eternal gain.
GONE BUT NOT FORGOTTEN.

A Memoriam Card. (© Bolton Council. From the Collection of Bolton Library and Museum Services)

Allied soldiers and medals struck to celebrate victories including the bombardment of the east coast, air raids on London and the sinking of the *Lusitania*.

In Britain the propaganda appeared with stereoscopic cards, which focused on the skeletal frames of the downed airships, Gothas, the bodies of the crews and the damaged caused.

The raids on the 25 and 26 September caused a total of £39,698 worth of damage; 43 people were killed, 31 were injured. No Zeppelins were shot down on this raid.

In Bolton, the air raid was used in an attempt to turn a conscientious objector at a local tribunal, who as a 33-year-old coal depot manager had been granted a temporary exemption from military service earlier in the year but had previously applied for exemption on grounds of conscience. The tribunal was chaired by Mayor James Seddon and other councillors.

The exchange:

Member:	You speak of sacredness of human life. What about those killed in air raids?
Man:	It would not help them if I went.
Member:	Yes, it would.
Member Two:	You recognise that if there were many like you the enemy would have greater scope and there might be more deaths.

Man:	If I could, I should be delighted to be a soldier, but I could not act against my own conscience.
Member Three:	If you went, it might help to prevent more of these things happening. Would you be prepared to sacrifice a little yourself to prevent others from being killed?
Man:	I would sacrifice my own life to prevent others being killed.
Chairman:	As the case has already been dismissed on conscientious grounds, it cannot be re-heard. Exemption refused, case dismissed.

The final GHQ report on the raid states that it was evident that the attack was intended against the Leeds manufacturing districts, as was reported by German communiqués, the area was approached and passed by four airships, L21 L22, L14 and L16. The other Zeppelins, L23 and L30 wandered off the Norfolk coast. The report notes these ships are notorious for 'Pusillanimous conduct' near British shores. L31 made a concerted effort on the Portsmouth area resulting in no great damage.

CHAPTER 10

L21 'THE DEATH OF "MARY"'

The autumn of 1916 was the zenith of the Zeppelins' freedom in the skies over England. Within a month the first airship to be destroyed in the air by an aircraft was SL11, which was shot down on 3 September by RFC pilot Leefe-Robinson. On 23 and 24 September, L32 (Peterson) and L33 (Bocker) were both shot down with the new ammunition near London. Then L31 commanded by Heinrich Mathy was shot down on 2 October at Potters Bar.

Eight weeks later in the last Zeppelin raid of 1916, the last Zeppelin to be over England was L21.

On 27 November, the weather had not been good for flying and Max Dietrich's 46th birthday celebrations were taking place at the *Kasino* at Nordholz with fellow commanders Frankenberg and Hollander of L21 enjoying a dish of salmon. Above the hubbub, the noise of the wind rattling the hall doors had quietened and the sun came through the windows. When the order to take off for Britain was received, Frankenberg apparently shouted, 'Leave the birthday decorations we'll celebrate tomorrow!' as the officers and their executive officers rushed from the table to their stations. Although, L21s Executive Officer Hans-Werner Salzbrunn

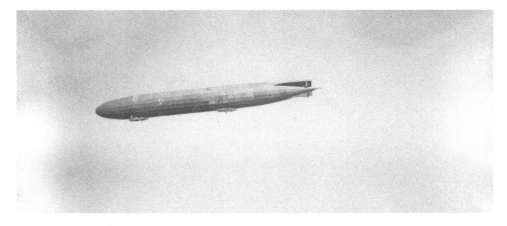

L21 on 14 November 1916.

had a premonition and soberly confided in his friend Richard Frey of L22 'I know we won't come back from this fight'.

A force of 10 Zeppelins took off with orders to target the Midlands and Tyneside. Over the North Sea, the raiders split into two groups – each heading for their designated target area. The raid proved to be a disaster for the Germans in more ways than one. The British defences in the towns of Hull, York, Howden, and Leeds all drove off Zeppelins with searchlights and AA fire.

Warnings had reached home defence squadrons of the northern raid at 10.15 p.m.

L34 under the command of Max Dietrich (L21's first commander) bombed Hartlepool, killing four people, followed shortly by *Kapitanleutnant* Erhlich's L35 a little after 11.30 p.m.

L34 was travelling at about 70 mph when it was caught in the searchlight at Castle Eden, north of the town. Second Lt Pyott of 36 Squadron RFC had been patrolling at 9,800 feet in his BE2c and sighted L34 at 11.30 p.m. He dived past, firing, aiming for points on the port side, after another few passes and a longer burst from his Lewis gun, he saw the tracer bullets penetrating the outer covering, suddenly causing an internal glare. Fire devoured the airship that was by now over the mouth of the Tees. It fell into the sea a mile off the Tees River, the intense heat scorching Pyott's face flying past, as the aluminium framework of L34 glowed red, sinking from the sky into the water. No survivors were found. Pyott had fired 71 rounds out of 97 from his Lewis gun's 'double' drum of ammunition.

This sight was visible to other Zeppelin crews, L35, 10 miles further north quickly gave up and retreated home. The crew of L22, 70 miles away in the Midlands raiding group, also witnessed the immolation of their comrades. No wonder Zeppelin crews were plagued by nightmares of burning airships: this highly visible slow death at such distance.

The British defence system used plotters to track the reported movements of raiders, and each one was given a girl's name. L21 on this raid was labelled 'Mary'. GHQ intelligence section later reported that L21's movements on this raid were the most interesting of any raider up to that point. Frankenberg had made landfall at Atwick at 9.20 p.m. and found that this raid was to be very different to the others. They were immediately fired on by AA guns at Barmston and, avoiding these, headed inland where aircraft were patrolling. Avoiding the marauding defence aircraft, L21 headed westward past Leeds, Barnsley and Macclesfield then heading for Cheshire and Staffordshire following the North Staffordshire Railway line. Passing south of Stockport, it went onwards to Kidsgrove and Goldenhill, where a steel furnace apparently was forced to show light to avoid an explosion, as well as Tunstall suffered a few bombs as at Chesterton, where there were ironstone burning hearths there was a concentrated bombardment. Then an area of collieries was attacked near Trentham and Fenton. No casualties were reported.

Heading for the coast, L21 appears to have had navigational and engine trouble taking a long weaving route that led them through a concentration of home defence airfields south-east of Nottingham.

Observers had deduced the path of the airship and had signalled that 'Mary is now going home'.

South of Grantham at 2.50 a.m. the searchlight at Buckminster 38 Squadron aerodrome RFC held L21 in its glare at about 7,000 feet. Capt. Birley flying a BE2e gave chase, following the ascending Zeppelin as it tried to escape the biplane.

After 25 minutes at 9,000 feet, Birley emptied two full drums of ammunition at L21 2,000 feet above him with no evident result.

Whilst keeping the aircraft level and changing the Lewis gun Magazine on its movable mount with freezing gloved fingers was inevitably distracting , and he lost sight of the Zeppelin. By this time L21 had risen to approximately 14,000 feet witnessed by another pilot at 3.00 a.m. 2nd-Lt DS Allan flying a BE2e at 12,000 feet had seen the tracer fire. It was here that the RFC pilots found that in their tractor biplanes the skilful evasive manoeuvring of Frankenberg and his crew meant they could not attack on a line.

The German crew must have desperately been pushing the Zeppelin to its limits for they knew, they had seen, they had dreamt what would happen if they didn't, they were flying for their lives. Freezing, exhausted and tested to the limit, they didn't give in against the strain, mechanical failure, navigational problems and now the hornet's nest of defence aircraft gravitating towards them in the darkness.

They now headed due east, adrenaline flowing and hearts beating faster – they kept going on slowly missing the Wash. After 4 a.m., they were spotted by Lt WR Gaynor from 51 Squadron RFC Marham flying over East Dereham in a FE2b, he pursued them to extreme firing range but his engine started to vibrate badly and misfire, shortly after cutting out leaving Gaynor to glide away from his quarry to a crash landing at Tibbenham.

The Maybach engines on board L21 had been running for over 15 hours, and the craft had been over England for nine hours and having been observed at multiple points to be drifting was. It has been since been assumed some technical problems were occurring. L21 passed north of Norwich, then over Wroxham steering south-east, reaching Great Yarmouth at 6 a.m. The official British report into this raid supposed that the timidity of Frankenberg was that he was concerned about his fuel supply and probably was heading for Belgium rather than northern Germany fearing the same fate as L19 and coming down in the sea. The crew of L21 had recently witnessed at distance the destruction of SL11 and L32.

Reported to have hovered at approximately 11,000 feet for seven minutes while turning on the prevailing wind, it drifted south-south-east over the sea but travelled parallel to the coastline into the sights of the AA battery at Bradwell.

However, the Battery searchlight and the Barr and Stroud height-finder were not operational due to the engine being allowed to cool down by the NCO in charge as to the point it could not be restarted in time. The skyline now was increasingly light so the ranges and heights were estimated.

They fired 17 rounds of high-explosive shell to no visible effect, but this did attract the attention of pilots patrolling the area. Flt Lt E Cadbury flying a BE2c took off in the direction of L21 now heading out to sea. Also heading for the

Zeppelin were Flt-sub-Lts GWR Fane and EL Pulling, both flying BE2c's. Just off the coast, it was thought that L21 was drifting without power until heading away from the coast descending to 8,000 feet.

At this point, the Bradwell Battery opened up at an estimated range of 16,000 yards firing five rounds to no obvious result.

Here roughly 6 miles off Lowestoft, early on the morning of Tuesday, 28 November, at about 6.35, L21 and her brave crew found that their luck had run out.

On board L21, the sense of relief must have been increasing as they headed for home; as long as the engines held out and the weather stayed fine they will be home nearer to warmth, wives, lovers, children, food and bed. The shattering of these by a strained shout from a lookout and the stuttering of a machine gun.

Achtung Flugzeug

Cadbury was first to reach L21, which was then at 8,200 feet, firing into the stern from 700 feet below to the gondola gunner's great frustration, as he attracted their considerable attention from a blind spot.

> Inside the Gondolas must have been frantic scenes, Telegraphs switched up to flank speed, quick orders ... elevator up ... rise ... rise ... rise ... – steer due east. Officers leaning out of the open side ports to see the situation for themselves ... Frantic orders into the speaking tubes – dump ballast ... shouted and lost amidst the noise of the MG08's return fire and the empty cartridges hitting the frozen floor around the gunner's feet as they swung the guns on the mounts to get aim on the attackers. One can only imagine the thoughts going through the minds of those working inside under and amid the girders, bracing wires fuel tanks and gas cells. The machinists working amid the noise of firing and engines kept pushing them to the limit ...

Cadbury fired off four drums of ammunition into the rear of L21 whose speed increased from 35 to 55 knots. This is described by Cadbury in a television interview for the BBC's 1964 series *The Great War*. Fane moved in as well attempting to shoot the starboard side but his gun had frozen due to being airborne since 4.35 a.m. He gained altitude to try to drop a bomb onto the top. Pulling flew underneath at about 50 feet distance firing two reported shots (but possibly up to 10) before his gun jammed, and he flew sharply to Starboard to clear it but moving into the sights of the gunners.

The fire meant the nightmare was becoming a reality, and the crew now faced those questions they had hoped they never would – to jump or stay and burn?

At this point, L21 was clearly on fire by the stern and as Fane flew across the top, it was burning and up at an angle of 45 degrees, the inferno spreading upwards, a gunner on the top gun-pit ran to the side and jumped off preferring to fall rather than stay in the fire.

Pulling reported that she was visibly foreshortened as fire devoured the fabric, the pilots flew around the dying Zeppelin. Fane apparently flew so close, he scorched his helmet and aircraft skin.

They died hard though, the German gunners determined to take one of the attackers with them were still firing, as L21 sank from the sky into the sea, a long candle of flame from the sky to the water. Pulling reported that the propellers were still turning as she fell. It took little over a minute for L21 to fall into the sea to sink immediately. There were no survivors.

The comment about seeing the Zeppelin 'considerably foreshortened' due to the fire spreading along the interior and eating away the external fabric; this effect can be seen in the cine films of the destruction of the Hindenburg many years later. Pulling's report indicates that Naval authorities located the site where L21 sank – 6 miles due east of Lowestoft, marked by a large area of oil-covered water and a shattered propeller blade where it had disappeared beneath the surface.

Pulling also reported that Cadbury and Fane attacked the Zeppelin without success, he attacked the Zeppelins underside that started to burn after two rounds, five minutes after Cadbury's attack finished and Fanes gun had jammed immediately. Seeing the ignition of the stern, it would be reasonable to say that Cadbury's drums of ammunition had ignited the gas cells.

Subsequently Pulling was awarded the DSO as at that point having flown 13 anti-Zeppelin sorties, the most of any RNAS or RFC pilot, whereas Cadbury and Fane received DSCs.

It is possible the reports were open to misconception and exaggeration; however, the facts remain that it was still dark. This would offer different impressions of L21 to the pilots who were at varying heights and distances around it. A claim was put in by the Bradwell Battery that they hit their target but it wasn't substantiated.

Sub Lt E L Pulling & Lt Cadbury. (© Trustees of the National Museum of the Royal Navy)

Sub Lt G. W. R. Fane in the cockpit of an F4 Martinsyde Buzzard 1918. (© Trustees of the National Museum of the Royal Navy)

CHAPTER 11

PULLING'S REPORT

At 6 a.m. I had descended to 6000 feet preparatory for landing when I saw anti-Aircraft guns in the direction of [Great] Yarmouth firing. I immediately steered a course southeast hoping to intercept their target at sea ... At 6:10 I sighted a Zeppelin making out to sea and proceeded in pursuit, having by this time reached the height of 8000 feet. A few moments later I saw an attack being made on her by a machine, which I was unable to see, the tracer ammunition was clearly visible ... About five minutes after the attack ceased I came level with the Zeppelin at 8300 feet, approaching her at right angles on her port quarter. I then turned sharply to the left and passed about 50 feet beneath her, firing as I did so. The Lewis gun fired two shots (both hitting), and stopped, and she immediately opened fire with a machine gun, apparently from the Gondolas. I turned sharply to the right intending to keep out of range until I had cleared the jam. A few seconds later on looking over my shoulder, I saw that the Zeppelin was on fire by the stern ... By this time I was to the southeast of the Zeppelin and apparently a good target against the dawn, for the fire was kept up for several seconds after she was alight ... I flew parallel to the Zeppelin for a short time a few hundred yards to the starboard of her, and watched her sink by the tail and dive into the sea. The flames spread with great rapidity. I was unable to discern any number on the airship as she was between my machine and the light. As I dived under her I noticed her propellers working and also two black crosses, one on each side of her stern. During the greater part of the operations she was canted up at an angle, which finally reached about 45 degrees. Thus at the moment of passing under her she appeared to me considerably foreshortened ... After witnessing the fall of the Zeppelin I steered due west hitting the coast about two miles north of Southwold. I steered due north to Yarmouth and landed there at 7:12am. I am uncertain as to the locality in which the Zeppelin fell but it appeared to me about 10 miles east of Lowestoft ... speed of the Zeppelin at the moment of attacking was about 55 knots. Air 1/721/59/12/1.

POETIC JUSTICE: FRIGHTFUL END OF EMISSARIES OF "FRIGHTFULNESS."

An artist's impression of L21's demise from the perspective of an armed trawler crew who witnessed the attack. Fane can be seen doing a celebratory loop to the left of the Zeppelin. (Courtesy of the National Museum of the Royal Navy)

Pulling's Be2c 8626 with RNAS ground crew – the Lewis gun on a flexible mount can be seen in front of the rear cockpit to be aimed upwards when flying under the Zeppelin. (© Trustees of the National Museum of the Royal Navy)

At this point it is reasonable to include this account of what occurred inside a dying Zeppelin, a terrifying situation to be in and as very few people survived, survivors' stories are virtually non-existent.

Heinz Ellerkamm, who in 1917 was the chief engineer artificer on the starboard engine car of L48 survived such a nightmarish inferno, having left the engine car to check the fuel *Benzine* tanks in the main Zeppelin body:

> I climbed the 13 rungs of the ladder in my heavy fur overcoat and huge felt overshoes, it was nasty at 30 below zero! On the middle rung of the ladder with the black depths below me and sky above ...I heard in the distance the creepy rattle of machine guns ... 25 shots ... just as I was about to enter the catwalk I heard a longer volley. It gave me a nasty, shivery sensation for any one shot could cause an explosion ... Suddenly I saw tiny blue flames appear in the fifth and sixth bags (gas cells) aft. Oh Lord! ... The roar of a mighty explosion ... I can still see the rigger racing through the gangway to the control car. Behind me and in front of me there were flames – bright red flames that danced about getting bigger and fiercer. I sensed the ship begin to drop. At this point we were at 4000 metres (13,123 feet). Slowly the ship dipped by the stern ... a sudden jerk and the L48 shot downwards ... I had a hard job to hold on to one of the girders in the passage way ... flames were dancing ... licking at my fur overcoat ... it was quite clear to me that it was no good trying to save myself ... some 10 or 12 ships had already been shot down in flames over England with no survivors ... the ship crashing down at a terrific rate and the air whistled as she cut her way through it ... the gas bags were burning away like mad ...
>
> ...When a flame catches the gold-beaters skin of a bag, it makes a frizzling sound just like a greasy bit of paper when you throw it in the fire ... we were whizzing like a streak of lightning ... the draught was driving the flames to port ... I was on the starboard side-walk ... the heat through my leggings ... falling falling falling ... we had often discussed this at Nordholz ... only one thing to do, get out! Jump for it! Don't stop to be burnt alive! ... suddenly the ships stern crashed to pieces ... I only knew that a chaotic jumble of girders, bracing wires and fittings were coming down on my head and above me a sea of flames was collapsing ... imprisoned in a cage, the bars of which were glowing red hot mass, my fur coat was burning ... the quickest way out was to starboard and with all my strength that such a moment of despair gives one, another girder gave way ... I crawled along the ground felt grass, behind me a mass of burning ... I rolled over 2 or 3 times then I found myself in the open air, 3 metres from the burning debris ... I can still see that meadow with horses and a duck flying overhead.

Ellerkamm found out years later that the officer of the watch *Leutnant* Mieth also had survived.

The horrific footage of the Hindenburg in 1937 at Lakehurst New Jersey shows the spread and speed of the fire, destruction and scale. If you watch the British Pathe you get the screams of the witnesses, see the destruction. People jumping and being crushed by the inferno. The Herb Morrison footage you will see from different perspectives, though with Morrison's incredibly emotional narration of what he is witnessing – 'It's burst into flames, its falling … oh the humanity … I can't talk any more Ladies and Gentlemen … it's just a mass of fucking wreckage … the worst thing I have ever witnessed'.

In October 1917, six Zeppelins were severely damaged and wrecked by weather returning from a raid over the English Channel, the mighty airships that had enraptured the pre-war populations had by now slipped from favour and were relegated to occasional use. Gothas were lighter, faster but inherently unstable after dropping the bomb-load. Therefore, targets or areas could be attacked with not much more accuracy but for a lot less monetary cost. On one raid over London, 26 were seen flying above the capital.

Flt Sub Pulling was killed with his passenger Flt Sub Lt Northrop on 2 March 1917 while doing a loop in the aircraft he had flown against L21. At 2,000 feet, the lower starboard wing failed while going upward at 45 degrees, the wing buckled and the BE2c fell to earth. He is buried in Great Yarmouth Cemetery in the Parish of Caister on Sea.

Cadbury survived the war to eventually attain the rank of Air Commodore and was knighted. Taking over the Cadbury company overseeing the merger between Cadbury's and J.S Fry & Sons. He died in 1967.

The young Sub Lt Fane, who had enlisted in the RNAS underage, cutting short his education at Charterhouse ended the war as a captain and lived until 1979.

Lancashire had not seen the last of Zeppelins after the 1916 raid, L61 paid a visit to Wigan, in April 1918, killing five people. As a newer ship, L61 had great climbing abilities and could reach much higher altitudes avoiding the defences. As Flight Commanders both Cadbury and Fane flew defensive sorties in DH9 aircraft against this raid to no success.

Fixed-wing aircraft caused more death and destruction than the Zeppelins had managed to do for a fraction of the cost to the Germans but without the sinister reputation of the Zeppelins. Statistically from 1915 to 1918: 1,414 people were killed in aerial attacks (557 approximately by airships) nationally and 3,416 wounded (1,358 by airships) by raids, approximately 8,500 bombs (5,806 by airships) were dropped on Great Britain.

There had been 54 airship raids in total: 1915 – 20;1916 – 23; 1917 – 7; 1918 – 4. The significant drop in numbers illustrates that the expense of putting these weapons up over a country now prepared was not worth the expense in lives, experience and machinery. In all, airship raids caused £1,537,585 worth of damage: £850,109 of this was in the London area, and of this £650,787 was caused by Mathy in two raids on the capital.

By 1918, German towns were being bombed by the Independent Bombing Force, a British bomber unit under Hugh Trenchard operating independently of the RFC or RNAS but not in the widespread way the Zeppelins had done to Britain, these were much smaller raids targeting aerodromes and small towns though not to any

Armistice Day 1918 – Victoria Square Bolton. (© Bolton Council. From the Collection of Bolton Library and Museum Services)

great scale on industry. Approximately 550–600 tons of bombs were dropped. These caused response raids over French towns and cities.

The final Zeppelin raid was on 5 August 1918.

L70 was the flagship of the Imperial German Naval Airship fleet leading the attack on England of L53, L56, L63 and L65. Aboard L70 was *FregettanKapitan* Peter Strasser, *Fuhrer der Luftschiffe* (Leader of Airships).

L70 had a ceiling of 21,000 feet as well as seven engines with a range of 7,000 miles. It was armed with 20 mm Oerlikon cannons instead of MG08s.

With a warning sent from a Lightship at sea, the Zeppelins with an uncharacteristic lack of caution flew towards the English coast in daylight as dusk approached. RAF pilots took off and headed out to sea, by 10.10 p.m. Maj. E. Cadbury flying a DH4 two-seat aircraft with Capt. Robert Leckie as his observer and gunner flew into the Zeppelins heading for the coast almost passing by L70. They turned and passing underneath Leckie fired his Lewis gun into the hull, turning the giant Zeppelin into an inferno that descended into the sea 8 miles off Wells on Sea.

Strasser had fulfilled the criteria in war for the most esteemed officer – you cannot ask people to die for your cause if you are not prepared to do so yourself.

He did so, at the head of his beloved airships on a raid against the enemy. He had enthusiastically contributed to the airship programme to the extent that his contribution was only superseded by the role of Count von Zeppelin.

On 7 August, L70 was discovered to be lying in 48 feet of water and raised in parts by the Royal Navy, to be analysed and searched. The investigators found documents relating to every Zeppelin raid of the war and the new technology aboard. Much was discovered about the most modern type of Zeppelin, mechanical details and its construction. The crew that were found in the Gondolas after medical investigation were said to have drowned – the crew including Strasser were all buried at sea.

The German airship services greatest achievement is perhaps not one of destruction, but of distraction. By December 1916, 17,340 officers and men were in the AA service, together with 12 RFC squadrons comprised of 200 officers, 2,000 other ranks and 110 aircraft for home defence duties. By 1918, there were 55 home squadrons. The threat of bombing reduced numbers of effective squadrons and trained pilots at the front from the urgency to have all any available squadrons based around the south and east, which otherwise would certainly have been at times not least during the German offensive of 21 March 1918. The mistakes and lessons learned by the British had been taken by the Germans as well and put these to effect use and ended the static trench warfare returning the war to that of manoeuvre, retreat and advance as in 1914.

Post-war, one of Germany's few remaining Zeppelins the Hindenburg had gained permission due to weather conditions to fly over England on 12 October 1936. Flying low on its return voyage from New York, the Hindenburg crossed the coast at Thornton-Cleveleys passing over Blackpool, Garstang, Burnley, Nelson, Bradford and Grimsby.

The last German Zeppelins *Graf Zeppelin* (LZ 127) and the *Graf Zeppelin II* (LZ 130) were dismantled in 1940 on the orders of Hermann Goering, their aluminium was melted down into aircraft parts for another war.

The once non-existent future of the Zeppelin has been returned with one of peaceful potential, the economical Zeppelin NT launched in 1997 has been somewhat of a success.

Facts appeared in the media about the NT after a flight over England in 2006, one such point was that in the regular use of the NT over one month resulted in the same usage of fuel that a Boeing 747 uses to taxi from an airport terminal to the runway before a take-off. Perhaps there is a future in the world of transport with the many protocols and treaties on carbon emissions, but its role in warfare as a front-line unit ended before the armistice of 11 November 1918.

Nowadays

In the areas affected by the raid, very little is left to show. The houses in Irwell Vale near the railway still bear pockmarked lintels. Holcombe village is probably the most visible reminder on the front of the old post office walls and lintels opposite the Shoulder of Mutton – now a private residence.

The Ramsbottom sites are all built upon, save for Bank Place at Pot Green that still stands.

In Bolton, the streets are still there but very few of the directly affected buildings survive. Lodge vale has gone but some of the mill ponds remain. Kirk Street was demolished in the 1960s for Bolton Institute now University. Holy Trinity Church is now apartments. Moor Mills still stands but the Parrot and Apple Street terraces are long gone. The Co-op Laundry was demolished in recent years and the land remains vacant. The surrounding structures of Town Hall were heavily redeveloped from the 1920s onwards and encircling streets, pubs and alleyways lost. Bessemers Forge on Moor Lane closed in 1924, and the site was cleared until the bus station was built at the end of the 1920s.

There is a painting by E. F. Skinner of a Bessemers works in Penistone, South Yorkshire, made during the First World War titled *Manufacturing Bessemer Steel* in the Science Museum Collection, London. It shows the reason for the glare that the works created and is worth seeing.

Holy Trinity church in July 2016. (© Scott Carter-Clavell)

L21.

The spinning mill element of Moor Mills in July 2016. (© Scott Carter-Clavell)

SELECT BIBLIOGRAPHY
AND SOURCES

J. Ali, *Our Boys* (Landy Publishing, 2007)

P. Annis, *Anti-Air Defences of the North* (Royal Air Force Historical Society, 1995)

C. Aspin, *Helmshore Historian* (1967)

T. Charman, *The First World War on the Home Front* (André Deutsch, 2014)

L. Chollet, *Balloon Fabrics Made Out of Goldbeater's Skins* (L'Aeronautique, 1922)

C. Cole and E. F. Cheesman, *The Air Defence of Great Britain 1914–1918*

Lt Col J. Craven-Hoyle, Ward Opening speech; Newhallhey Military Hospital, 14 October 1916

K. Frankenberg and Z. S. Oblt, Report. 26 September 1916 (Nordholz Aeronauticum)

M. Goldsmith, *Zeppelin A Biography* (W. Morrow & Co., 1931)

M. Goodwill and G. May, 'Zeppelins over Sheffield', http://www.brigantian. force9.co.uk

M. Hammerton, *The Zeppelin Menace, Perceptions & Responses 1907–16* (Royal Air Force Historical Society, 1995)

R. Jackson, *Air Defence against the Zeppelin 1915–17* (Royal Air Force Historical Society, 1995)

P. Klein, *Achtung! Bomben Fallen!* (Verlag von Koehler, 1934), http://m. archivgnoien.de.tl/L-21.htm

S. Longstreet, *Canvas Falcons* (Barnes & Noble, 1995)

L. Macdonald, *Somme* (Macmillan, 1983)

R. Marben, *Zeppelin Adventures* (John Hamilton, 1931)

J. Morris, *German Air-Raids on Great Britain 1914–1918* (Sampson Low, Marston & Co., 1925)

K. Poolman, *Zeppelins over England* (The Camelot Press, 1960)

D. H. Robinson, *The Zeppelin in Combat* (1994) p. 217 cit. Korvettenkapitan H. Hollender 'Die Deutschen Luftstreitkrafte Im Weltkrieg', ed. Georg Paul Neurmann (E. S. Mittler u. Sohn, 1920) p. 395

P. J. C. Smith, *Zeppelins over Lancashire* (Neil Richardson, 1991)
Van Emden and Humphries, *Voices from the Home Front* (2003)
D. Wood, *Air Defence in the North* (Royal Air Force Historical Society, 1995)

Newspapers, Periodicals and Reports
Air Raids 1916 (GHQ IS December 1916)
Bolton Evening News (26 September 1916)
Bolton Journal and *Guardian* (18 December 1918)
Burnley Express
Bury Guardian (September 1916)
Correspondence of Bradshaw Gass and Hope 1915–1918 (Bolton Archives)
Derby Street Mixed Board School Diary (Bolton Archives)
Derby Street Mixed Board School Log (Bolton Archives)
Diary of Thomas Sanderson (Bolton Archives)
Director of Air Services, Report on Ammunition Experiments at Kingsworth
    (National Archives: Air 1/567/16/15/119)
EL Pulling, *Report of L21 Destruction* (National Archives: Air 1/721/59/12/1)
Elizabeth Andersen interview with *Bolton Journal*, August 1973 – Newspaper
    Cuttings (Archives ref. B8 p. 202)
Flight, 25 September 1914/1 October 1915/28 September 1916
Lancashire Evening Post
New York Times (5 July 1908)
North West Sound Archive Catalogue (Bolton Archives: 1992)
Ramsbottom Observer (29 September 1916)
Rossendale Free Press 1916/1966/1976
Yorkshire Post